Compiled by Rabbi Daniel ✓ P9-DBU-770

LIVING ON

MESSAGES, MEMORIES AND MIRACLES FROM THE HAR NOF MASSACRE

First Edition December 2014

ISBN 978-1-68025-006-0
Copyright © 2014 by Rabbi Daniel Yaakov Travis

All questions and comments to the author
are welcomed at: dytravis@actcom.com
or 14/22 Agasi Street, Har Nof, Jerusalem Israel

DISTRIBUTED IN ISRAEL BY:
Kulmus Book Distribution

DISTRIBUTED BY:
Feldheim Publishers
POB 43163 / Jerusalem, Israel

208 Airport Executive Park
Nanuet, NY 10954
www.feldheim.com

Printed in Israel

Dedicated *le'ilui nishmas* the four *Kedoshim*
murdered *al Kiddush Hashem*
in Har Nof, Yerushalayim
25 Cheshvan 5775

Rabbi Avrohom Shmuel Goldberg, *Hy"d*
Rabbi Aryeh Kupinsky, *Hy"d*
Rabbi Kalman Ze'ev Levine, *Hy"d*
Rabbi Moshe Twersky, *Hy"d*

And for the *refuah sheleimah* of the injured
and in recognition of the many
Jews who have reached out
in *chessed* during this time

May all of *Klal Yisrael* continue
"Living On" in unity

Kislev 5775

On 25 Cheshvan 5775, four *kedoshim* were killed, wearing tallis and tefillin, in *beis hakenesses* Kehilat Bnei Torah in Yerushalayim's Har Nof neighborhood. All of *Klal Yisrael* mourned the untimely passing of these tzaddikim and strengthened themselves in *chessed*, unity, Torah, *tefillah* and many other areas. It is important that we do all we can to preserve the momentum that this tragic incident has generated.

Rabbi Daniel Yaakov Travis, *Rosh Kollel* of one of the *kedoshim*, and friend and neighbor of all of them, has taken upon himself the task of maintaining the momentum spurred by this event. Following a tragedy of this magnitude, many people are seeking direction and meaning in what took place. The book *Living On* draws from insights of *Gedolei Yisrael*, as well as personal accounts, to clarify the powerful messages that Hashem has sent us.

In this lucid presentation, the author reveals an authentic Torah perspective to guide the reader. We encourage everyone to study and absorb the poignant and timely message of this critically important work, and we extend to Rabbi Travis our *brachah* that he continue to inspire his fellow Jews. May he see true *hatzlachah* in all his endeavors.

Rav Yitzchak Berkovits – Rosh Reshes Hakollelim Linas Tzedek

Rav David Cohen – Rosh Yeshivas Chevron

Rav Reuven Elbaz – Rosh Yeshivas Ohr HaChaim

Rav Zalman Nechamia Goldberg –
    Former Rosh Av Beis Din of Yerushalayim

Rav Yaakov Hillel – Rosh Yeshivas Ahavat Shalom

Rav Shmuel Kamenetsky - Rosh Yeshivas Yeshivah of Philadelphia

Rav Tzvi Kushelevsky – Rosh Yeshivas Heichal HaTorah

Rav Zev Leff – Mara D'asra Moshav Matisyahu

Rav Naftali Nussbaum – Rosh Yeshivas Tchebin and Chayei Moshe

Rav Yisroel Reisman – Rosh Yeshivas Torah V'Daas

בכ"ה בחשון תשע"ה מתו על קידוש השם ארבעה קדושים — כשהם עטופים בטלית ועטורים בתפילין — בבית כנסת "קהילת בני תורה", הר נוף, ירושלים. כל עם ישראל היה שותף לאבל של משפחות צדיקים אלו, ורבים קיבלו קבלות והתחזקו בחסד, באחדות, בתורה, בתפילה ובמצוות אחרות. מוטל עלינו לעשות כמיטב יכולתנו להמשיך את ההתעוררות הרוחנית שבאה לאחר אירוע קשה זה.

הרב דניאל יעקב טרביס שליט"א, ראש כולל שבו למד אחד הקדושים, וידיד של כל ארבעתם, החליט לשמר את ההתעוררות שבאה בעקבות האסון. לאחר אסון נורא שכזה רבים מחפשים כיוון ודרך איך לנהוג לאור המצב. הספר "Living On" ("ממשיכים לחיות") מלקט מדבריהם של גדולי ישראל, כמו כן סיפורים אישיים של בני משפחות הקדושים, והפצועים, ושאר המתפללים. ובעזרתם הוא מנסה להבהיר את המסרים שה' שולח לנו.

בהצגת דברים אלה בצורה ברורה, הכותב מעניק לקורא השקפה תורנית טהורה שיש בה כדי לספק את ההדרכה הנחוצה. אנו מציעים לכולם ללמוד ולהפנים את המסר הנוגע לימינו אנו, על ידי יצירה חשובה זו. ברכותינו להרב טרביס שליט"א שימשיך להרבות תורה ויראה בישראל, ויזכה להצלחה רבה בכל מעשיו.

באנו ע"ז הח"מ

יצחק מרדכי הכהן רובין

רב ומו"ץ בהר נוף ירושלים

אב"ד בבד"ץ בנשיאות הגר"ן קרליין

בס"ד כסלו תשע"ה

הריני בזה בלב שבור ומורתח תוך ימי האבל וההספד על הני קדושי עליון הי"ד שנטבחו ונהרגו בידיים אכזריות ביום המר והנמהר כ"ה לחדש מרחשוון, ואשר עדיין הלב רועד ורוחת ממידת הדין שנמתחה על קהילתנו, ה' ירחם על כולנו.

והגה ברוחו הרה"ג היקר ר' דניאל יעקב טרויויס ראש כולל "תורת חיים", להעלות על הכתב דברי התעוררות וההספד שנאמרו בימי האבל הנורא, ובתוכו רצוף דברים במעלתם של הני קדושים הי"ד.

והנה אבל זה שאנו כואבים הוא אבל יחיד למשפחות השבורות ולבני קהילתנו, אך הוא גם אבל ציבור לכל ישראל, שנאמר שה פזורה ישראל, ודרשו חז"ל [ויקרא רבה פרשת ויקרא פרשה ד], נמשלו ישראל לשה מה שה הזה לוקה על ראשו או באחד מאבריו וכל אבריו מרגישין.

וכולנו שואלים מה זאת עשה ה' לנו, ודעת לנבון שהתשובה היחידה לזה היא, הצור תמים פעלו כי כל דרכיו משפט קל אמונה ואין עול צדיק וישר הוא, ואין דרך להבין מאורעות קשים מעין אלו, אלא באמונה שלימה שהכל מאתו יתברך, שעצתו אמונה ופעולתו אמת.

ויתכן שכל זאת באת לנו להחדיר ביתר שאת וביתר עוז, שהקב"ה מלוא כל הארץ כבודו, דבר שבדורות קודמים היה נחלת הכלל, ועתה בדורנו נחלש קימעא הרגש זה מרוב חדירת החומר, ופעמים שמאבדים את ההרגשה הפשוטה שיש מנהיג לבירה, וסומכים על כוחנו ועוצם ידנו. ודוקא בעקבות אסון נורא זה שהדרך היחידה להבין את הקורות אותנו, היא על ידי חיזוק האמונה, הוא גופא יביא לחזק את הידיעה היסודית שה' אלוקינו בקרבנו.

ברכתי ברכת כהן שקונטרס זה יביא התעוררות וחיזוק, להגיד כי ישר ה' צורי ולא עולתה בו.

וע"ז בעה"ח
בשברון לב

[חתימה]

[חותמת]

רח' שאולזון 62/9 הר נוף ירושלים 9540067   ת.ד. 43019   י-ם 9143001
טל: 02-6518525   פקס: 02-6516377

Contents

Rav Moshe Twersky *Hy"d*

MESSAGES

(in the order that they were received)

LIVING ON

Introduction

THE PROPHET YIRMIYAHU CRIED, *"Eini eini yordah mayim ki rachok mimeni menachem, meishiv nafshi* — My eyes, my eyes, stream with tears, for consolation is far from me" (*Eichah* 1:16). Rashi explains that the repetitive language indicates inconsolable weeping.

Crying usually helps a person express his grief and brings a feeling of relief of painful emotions. However, when a person feels immeasurable pain, he just keeps crying and crying and crying. This is what Rashi means: Even after so much crying, consolation is still far from me.

I do not believe that I ever cried so much in one day as I did on Tuesday, 25 Cheshvan — November 18, 2014. That was the day of the murder of the four *kedoshim* of Har Nof. The first *niftar* I heard about was Rav Aryeh Kupinsky, my next-door neighbor, a *yedid nefesh* who had learned together with me in yeshivah. Two years ago, his fourteen-year-old daughter passed away unexpectedly in her sleep. The family was just starting to get over the shock of losing their sister, and now their father is gone.

Afterwards, when I heard about Rav Moshe Twersky, who was a *maggid shiur* at Yeshivas Toras Moshe, where I studied for five years as a *bachur*, I cried even more.

Then I heard about Rav Avrohom Shmuel Goldberg, my son-in-law's cousin, who made *sheva brachos* for my daughter not long ago in his home, and I cried some more.

After these three doses of bad news in one morning, I thought I had exhausted my supply of tears.

At 1 p.m., I got a phone call from one of my *talmidim*, who told me that Rav Kalman Levine, a *rosh chaburah* and rebbi in our *kollel*, had been murdered. The tears began to flow again, stronger than ever. *My eyes, my eyes…*

Keeping the Momentum

THE PERIOD SINCE THE HAR NOF MASSACRE took place has been a time of introspection and elevation for those of us impacted by the tragedy. And countless Jews around the world felt the impact with force. We have witnessed an outpouring of *chessed* from Jews all over the world, and here in Israel *rabbanim* spoke every day about the message that we can take from this tragedy. All of us took to heart what happened in Har Nof, and the imprint that this event made on *Klal Yisrael* was clear.

However, time is the greatest enemy of momentum. If we do not make an effort to hold on to the impact, then we will almost inevitably lose whatever we have gained, and we will be back at square one. We need to keep the momentum going, and use this incident as an impetus to make progress toward the final redemption.

In *Tehillim*, Dovid Hamelech recounts numerous forms of miraculous salvations. The chapter concludes, "Who is the wise person who can preserve this, and thinks about Hashem's kindness" (*Tehillim* 107:34). Why does one need wisdom to thank Hashem, and what exactly are we preserving?

Rav Yitzchak Ezrachi (*Mizmor L'Sodah*, p. 186) explains that when a person sees the Hand of Hashem in his life he is momentarily inspired. Yet "preserving" these feelings is no simple matter and it requires great wisdom. Only deep contemplation of Hashem's miracles allows us to truly integrate what happened into ourselves. In this way, we can hold on to any positive momentum that is granted to us.

Hashem sent us a very strong message that morning in Har Nof. Woe to us if we neglect to study its message in depth and, to the best of our abilities, try to understand what He is telling us. If we are able to hear the deeper message of the Almighty, we will inevitably make changes in our lives. This will bring us closer and closer to the final redemption.

Changing Ourselves

RAV YISRAEL SALANTER ONCE COMMENTED that it is more difficult to change a single personality trait than to master the entire Talmud. All of us are familiar with the truth of this comment. What is the secret of overcoming this obstacle?

Rav Yitzchak Greenberg, a close disciple of the Chazon Ish, once remarked that changing oneself is really not so hard. The difficulty is in deciding that making a transformation is a top priority in one's life and that one really wants to change. After the decision to change has become crystal-clear in one's mind, then the actual change is not so difficult.

Rav Yitzchak Mordechai Rubin, the Rav of Kehilat Bnei Torah in Har Nof, where the incident took place, spoke at the *levayah* of the *kedoshim* and made reference to the *passuk* (*Mishlei* 14:10), "*Lev yode'a maras nafsho,*" The heart recognizes its true nature. Deep down inside, each of us knows what Hashem wants and expects of us. No one knows your most profound challenges better than you do yourself. Each of us can identify which of these areas we should focus our efforts on. If we use what happened to clarify this and to face these challenges head-on, then we have heard the message that Hashem was conveying to us.

"Living On"

IN ORDER TO FULLY ABSORB THE IMPACT OF THE Har Nof Massacre in a constructive way, there are three things we must do.

1. As explained earlier, Hashem's actions only influence us if we give thought to what took place. If we do not contemplate Hashem's Hand in this incident, we are likely to lose the momentum that was so strong when it happened. This book reveals the inside story of the tragedy in a way that has not been presented anywhere else before, with the cooperation of many people who were there and directly affected.

2. We must have a clear picture of who these *kedoshim* were, and perhaps some clues as to why they were chosen from among all Jews to die *al kiddush Hashem*. So too, we must empathize with the pain of the *almanos*, *yesomim*, relatives, friends and neighbors, who feel the sudden loss of these beloved Jews so keenly. Only after we have done this can we really appreciate the devastating nature of what happened, and what a great loss it was to *Klal Yisrael*. This book introduces you to these special tzaddikim through the eyes of those who knew and appreciated their unique qualities.

3. After we have recognized that Hashem's Hand enacted this and how devastating was His decree, we need guidance from the *Gedolim* and great *talmidei chachamim* of our generation: What are we meant to learn

from this event? Which areas should we consider rectifying? What can we do to forestall another tragedy like this, *Rachmana litzlan*? This book gathers insights and messages from some of the leading lights of our time, providing us with clarity and direction in these dark and confusing times.

Living On is your guidebook through the maze of dark feelings and questions toward a place of hope and elevation.

Through this book, the *kedoshim* are *Living On* in our memories as shining examples of what a Jew can be. The momentum generated by the massacre is *Living On* as each of us try to make meaningful use of its impact. And we, the Jewish people, are *Living On* and coming ever closer to the redemption, despite the pain and hardships of our times.

Acknowledgments

Hapa'am Odeh es Hashem I FEEL IMMENSE GRATITUDE TO THE Almighty and everyone involved with this *sefer* for getting such a work out so quickly. The idea for this book came during a Shabbos *seudah* discussion with Dr. Binyamin Surovsky. We felt that following such a tragic event, and in light of our personal connection to the *kedoshim*, something major had to be done to preserve the momentum that had been generated. By the next *erev Shabbos*, the book was already written, edited and on its way to print. Anyone who knows anything about the usually interminable process of book publishing must acknowledge the Divine assistance we merited.

There are a number of people who set aside other commitments and devoted great time and energy to make this project successful.

Mrs. Naomi Elbinger did much of the writing and research, as well as guiding and managing the direction of the book. She wishes to thank her husband, Rabbi Shmuel Elbinger, and their children for their support during this project.

Mrs. Sara Chava Mizrahi showed exceptional dedication and readiness to do whatever it took to bring this book to reality. Her superior editing skills raised this book to worldclass standard in a short time.

Mrs. Miriam Jakubowicz, Mrs. Simcha Ashkenazi, Mrs. Paula Weinberg, Mrs. Devorah Rachmani, Mrs. Sara

Ackman and Mrs. Yael Goldwasser helped transcribe, proofread and translate for *Living On*. Mrs. Eden Chachamtzedek did a beautiful job laying out this book. All of these professionals worked long hours and put aside other projects because they believed in the significance of this project.

I must also express my appreciation to all of my *talmidim* in Kollel Toras Chaim, especially Rabbi Chaim Burman and Rabbi Yosef Chaim Eidenson, who spent a significant amount of time working on this manuscript, and Rabbi Shmuel Kaffe for once again producing stunning graphics. A great thanks goes to Yotzei L'Ohr Printers, who organized the production of this *sefer* quickly, and to R' Eli Hollander of Feldheim and R' Avishai of Kulmus distribution who helped distribute this *sefer*.

A special thanks goes to the many *rabbanim* whose *hespedim* and *drashos* were used in this *sefer*, especially Moreinu U'Rabbeinu Maran Rav Moshe Sternbuch, *shlita*, Rosh Yeshivah and Rosh Av Beis Din of Yerushalayim; and Rav Yitzchak Mordechai Rubin, *shlita*, Mara D'asra Kehilat Bnei Torah, where the Har Nof Massacre took place. I also thank my personal Roshei Yeshivos, Rav Tzvi Kushelevsky, *shlita*, Rosh Yeshivas Heichal HaTorah; and Rav Moshe Meiselman, *shlita*, Rosh Yeshivas Toras Moshe, whom I am also privileged to have as my neighbors in Har Nof. May they all have *arichus yamim* and *shanim* and *nachas* from all of their *talmidim* and children.

Thank you to the various eyewitnesses and primary sources who added details and helped verify the accuracy of the story, including: Rabbi Shmuel Goldstein, Rabbi Motti Oderberg, Rabbi Joe Werfel, Rebbetzin Tziporah Heller,

Mrs. Chaya Tavin, Mrs. Tamar Ansh, Mrs. Miriam Shaul and numerous others.

Finally, I must thank my family, who made space for me during this time to help me get this *sefer* out: my son-in-law Rabbi Avraham Dovid Michael Salasnik and my daughter Nechama Rachel, and my son Chaim Yitzchak. *Acharon, acharon chaviv,* I thank my *eishes chayil* Nomi Bracha; all that I have is hers.

Above all I have a debt of thanks to the Almighty, Who has helped and guided me constantly, from the moment I was born until today. Since my life was saved in a near-fatal car crash over twenty-two years ago on Chai Sivan, 5752, I have had the privilege to be the Rosh Kollel of Kollel Toras Chaim for eleven years and to publish many *sefarim* in English and *lashon hakodesh.* My only request is that He continue to shower His Kindness on me and all of *Klal Yisrael* by bringing the final redemption quickly.

Rabbi Daniel Yaakov Travis
18 Kislev 5775
Jerusalem, Israel

MIRACLES

"The first thing I said when I woke up was the passuk
'Ashirah laHashem bechayai, I will sing to Hashem
with my life' (Tehillim 104:33). Even though it
is looked at as a very bad story, there are
so many miracles that Hashem did."

– Rabbi Shmuel Goldstein

About Kehilat Bnei Torah

H AR NOF IS A RELIGIOUS NEIGHBORHOOD ON THE WEST-ern edge of Jerusalem. The first residents moved there in the early 1980s, and it is now home to around 20,000 residents and dozens of shuls.

Near the hairpin intersection of Agassi and Katzenellenbogan Streets, in the upper part of the neighborhood, is a large shul named Kehilat Bnei Torah. The shul community has existed for twenty-seven years, ever since its Rabbi, Harav Yitzchak Mordechai Hakohen Rubin, *shlita*, was invited to be its spiritual leader. For many years, the congregants davened in a temporary location down the street, and the current building itself was opened only eleven years ago.

The Kehilat Bnei Torah building is a well-designed structure with four levels: below ground is a social hall; the entrance level, reached by climbing a few steps, houses the entrance hall, the rabbi's office, and a *beis medrash* used for minyanim and for learning Torah — this is the "downstairs *beis medrash*" that was targeted by the terrorists; the first floor houses the main shul, which is much larger than the downstairs one; and the top floor is the ladies' gallery. As such, it is not just a shul, but a Torah center that serves the entire community and neighborhood.

Bnei Torah prides itself on being a community institution, with more than 200 member families and another 200 families associated with the shul in various ways.

The community welcomes anyone who considers themselves to be *bnei Torah* — Jews committed to mitzvos and Torah learning, be they Ashkenazi or Sephardi; whether they work or learn in *kollel* or do both; whether they are native Israelis or immigrants from any country in the world. Congregants include prominent *rabbanim* and Roshei Yeshivah from the world's most famous Torah families, as well as "regular" working Jews who do their best to make Torah a priority despite their busy schedules.

At Bnei Torah, everyone davens side by side.

The community has a strong emphasis on tolerance and mutual acceptance, and a strict "no *machlokes* allowed" policy. Bnei Torah is run entirely by volunteers, including the rabbi himself.

Rabbi Rubin is now considered one of the pre-eminent rabbis of Har Nof, and many people consult with him from outside the Bnei Torah community. He serves as a *dayan* in the *beis din* of Rabbi Nissim Karelitz, *shlita*, and is famous for his books on various topics in halachah, such as *Orchos Shabbos*.

Bnei Torah is a vibrant community hub, with learning sessions, minyanim and events going on from early in the morning until late into the night.

The shul was already bustling with people, both upstairs and downstairs, before the massacre started on 25 Cheshvan 5775.

THE STORY:
From the Outside and from the Inside

The News Report THE 25TH OF CHESHVAN/NOVEMBER 18, 2014 was an ordinary Tuesday morning in the Jerusalem neighborhood of Har Nof. At Kehilat Bnei Torah, a local shul located on Agassi Street, close to thirty people were in the midst of the *amidah* of the 6:25 a.m. *Shacharis* minyan in the small downstairs *beis medrash*. Silence reigned, as each congregant was immersed in his own quiet prayer, wrapped in tallis and tefillin.

6:57 a.m.: Two Arab terrorists entered the shul building via the main entrance, shouting, "Allahu Akbar" (G-d is great). They fired their first round of bullets on their way in, mortally wounding Rabbi Kalman Levine, Hy"d, who was standing in the entrance hall.

6:59 a.m.: After hearing the sounds of gunfire and shouting, some of the worshippers fled the shul through a side door, before the terrorists entered the sanctuary. Others were too stunned or too far from the side exit to escape. They took cover under the tables. After the terrorists burst into the shul itself, they immediately shot Rabbi Avrohom Shmuel

21

Goldberg, Hy"d, and Rabbi Moshe Twersky, Hy"d, both of whom were positioned on the left side of the room.

7:02 a.m.: The remaining congregants attempted to take cover as the terrorists continued to shoot indiscriminately. One 16-year-old boy threw a chair at the terrorists and then managed to flee. Other congregants hurled tables and shtenders. Rabbi Aryeh Kupinsky, Hy"d, tried to fight them, while calling out to the others: "Everybody, run!" He was killed in the process.

7:05 a.m.: The gunfire paused. The terrorist's gun had jammed and he struggled to fix it. During that pause, about fourteen more people fled. Meanwhile, the second terrorist attacked individual congregants with a meat cleaver. About eleven Jews were left in the shul, four of them dead or mortally wounded, most of the others with injuries of different kinds.

7:08 a.m.: Two policemen burst into the building, leading to a gunfight with the terrorists.

7:11 a.m.: The two terrorists had been shot dead at the entrance by the policemen, one of whom was also mortally wounded. Emergency personnel entered the shul to tend to the wounded.

The Inside Story

THERE WERE COUNTLESS NEWS REPORTS broadcast throughout the world about what happened that Tuesday morning in Kehilat Bnei Torah. Some major international news outlets reported the story with outrageous inaccuracy and bias. Israel-based and Jewish news sources were certainly more sympathetic and interested in the truth, though sometimes controversially graphic and sensationalist.

One thing is for certain: None were completely accurate in their reporting. In writing this book, we have tried our best to be as accurate as possible in describing the details of the incident, relying on multiple reports and giving the manuscript to eyewitnesses for review.*

Besides a commitment to accurate reporting, there was something else missing from the majority of news reports. Let's call it "a view through the eyes of *emunah*." As Jews, we believe that all is from Hashem, both the bitter and the sweet. To really grasp the inside story, the details are very important, as are the individual experiences of those touched by this drama. But our perspective matters most of all.

This book attempts to tell this story as it has not been told before: with consciousness of Hashem's Guiding Hand every step of the way.

As gruesome as the news reports were, in the aftermath it became clear that there were countless instances of *chessed*, courage and Divine intervention in this story. It was a morning of many miracles, and though we will probably never fully understand His reasons, the more we know about what happened that morning, the more the precision of His Will becomes apparent.

There were no coincidences.

---

* Some aspects of the story remain unclear despite our efforts to clarify them, and some reports contradict each other. We humbly ask the *mechilah* of anyone who feels that we did not report the events as he experienced them.

Before the Minyan

I PERSONALLY DAVENED WITH THE 6:25 A.M. Bnei Torah minyan every morning for years and felt a deep connection and friendship with all the regulars. I can vividly imagine the scene of them all arriving and wrapping themselves in tallis and tefillin that Tuesday morning, as I have seen them do countless times.

After the tragedy, many people recounted how they planned and wished to be part of the 6:25 minyan at Bnei Torah that day, but strange circumstances beyond their control held them back.

For example, Rabbi Akiva Neuwirth, son of the renowned author of *Shemiras Shabbos K'Hilchasah,* was a regular in that minyan. He was usually on time, but on that day he found himself a few minutes late as he walked up the stairs to Bnei Torah. Recalling how his father strongly cautioned against being late for davening, the younger Rabbi Neuwirth turned around to find another minyan.

On the other hand, the first victim to lose his life, Rabbi Kalman Levine, never prayed weekday *Shacharis* at Bnei Torah, though he did daven there at other times. That Tuesday morning, he had already davened *neitz* at a different shul. It was highly unusual for him to be at Bnei Torah at that hour. He had only come in order to ask the shul's rabbi, Rav Yitzchak Mordechai Rubin, *shlita,* an urgent *she'eilah.*

For that reason, he was standing outside the *beis medrash* in the entrance hall, near the door to the Rav's study, making him the first target as the terrorists entered the building.

Rabbi Levine came at that time because Rav Rubin habitually davens at the 7 a.m. minyan upstairs, arriving a few minutes early to wrap himself in tallis and tefillin in his office. However, by the time Rav Rubin arrived that day the commotion had already started — so he did not enter the building. Instead of encountering Rav Rubin, who is usually in the entrance hall just before 7 a.m., they encountered Rabbi Levine, who is never in that place at that time.

What is clear from these chilling true stories is that we cannot understand why one person is seemingly saved by a mitzvah, while another loses his life in pursuit of a mitzvah. There is no way to understand the whys of Divine Providence. But that does not mean that these stories should be dismissed, or called "coincidences."

Rather, they illustrate so clearly that all is from Hashem. Things that seem "likely" and "logical" do not eventuate, while the "unexpected" and "impossible" take place instead.

The mass media coverage presented the Har Nof Massacre as gruesome and depressing. Graphic images of the carnage and grief flooded our senses, causing us to want to turn our faces away from it.

Though pain and horror are natural, necessary reactions to this atrocity, to dwell only on those aspects is to take a surface view. As Jews, we must always look deeper at the painful aspects of life, to see the message and meaning. One of the reasons we wrote this book is to help you see a different side of the story that unfolded that morning in Har Nof — the inside story.

Read these accounts and notice how an unlikely chain of events brought certain people to certain places at certain times — and all of them met very particular fates. The more we understand this clearly, the more we fulfill the verse in *Devarim* (4:35): "You have been shown, in order to know, that Hashem, He is the G-d. There is nothing besides Him."

Ein Od Milvado — There is nothing besides Him.

There are so many stories from that morning that illustrate this point with blinding clarity.

Listen closely as Chaya Tavin, a resident of nearby Katzenellenbogen Street, shares her family's story of that morning:

My husband Yaakov came home to get our son, Binyomin Dovid, ready for the school bus. You see, Tuesday morning is "Abba day." Binyomin Dovid looks forward to Tuesday morning all week, maybe because Abba puts ketchup on the cheese sandwich, or puts more pretzels in the bag than Ima does, or more salt on the salad. Or maybe because he so loves his *abba* and their special morning together.

Since Tuesday is their special day, my husband davens at the *neitz* minyan next to our house, instead of his regular 6:25 minyan in Kehilat Bnei Torah. My husband might have gone to his regular minyan anyway. Since he was often the only *kohen*, on Tuesdays he would pop in for *chazaras hashatz* just to *duchen* for them. The carnage occurred during *chazaras hashatz*.

But Hashem had other plans for my husband. A few months ago a member of the shul, a *kohen*, became an *avel* (a mourner) and he asked my husband if he could be the regular *baal tefillah*. This Tuesday my husband did not pop in to *duchen*, because he knew there would be another *kohen* in his minyan. So after *neitz* at HaGra Shul, where he had met his friend Rabbi Kalman Levine, he came home. He was safe at home while the massacre unfolded at his usual shul down the block.

Later that day, between the hope and the tears, my husband and I remembered a story from long ago. Binyomin Dovid was a sickly baby with Down syndrome and a host of medical issues. I needed *chizuk*. I made my way to Bnei

Brak to see Rebbetzin Kanievsky. I waited outside until it was my turn. I then came in to her, a sleeping baby in my arms. Rebbetzin Kanievsky took one look at him and said, "You don't know what *shemirah* (protection) you have in your home."

I thought I understood at the time. Perhaps, I thought, other things would be easier because this would be difficult. But now, almost thirteen years later, I truly understand what Rebbetzin Kanievsky meant. Binyomin Dovid was the only reason my husband was not with his regular minyan that morning.

Moreover, my husband's post-davening *chavrusa* was also a stalwart regular in that minyan. But since he knew that my husband was spending time with our son that morning, he also decided to daven elsewhere for a change.

We could not have imagined so many years ago that our son would perhaps save his father's life and the life of his *chavrusa*.

Another local resident's remarkable story was written up by his neighbor, the writer Tamar Ansh*:

First, some back story. I have a learning *seder* early in the morning, before going to my set *sedarim* each day, and my schedule is very precise. This first *seder* is at 7:30 a.m., by telephone, as my *chavrusa* lives in Ramot. Because of this, I must daven at the 6:25 a.m. minyan, and my *makom kevua* for this davening is by Kehilat Bnei Torah.

However, as on time as I normally am, we are all human

---

* Excerpted from an article by Tamar Ansh, originally published in *Hamodia*.

and it can sometimes happen that I am a few minutes late. I've had a *she'eilah* for a while already about what to do if I do happen to be late. Should I simply rush through *Pesukei D'zimra* in order to catch up to the minyan and be on time, or if there is not enough time for even that, should I skip over some and make them up later? If I daven in the next minyan, which starts at 7:00, I will be late for my early-morning learning. Perhaps it's better to have more of the *limud Torah* instead. Which is better?

A few weeks ago I decided to ask my *she'eilah* to Harav Ezriel Auerbach, *shlita*. I'd thought about the *she'eilah* from several angles and was fairly certain the Rav would tell me that being on time for Torah learning is more important. That's why the Rav's answer really took me by surprise.

Harav Auerbach listened carefully to what I had to say. Without hesitating for a second, he wagged his finger and declared, "*Ledaleg zeh lo hamehalach* — Skipping [over *Pesukei D'zimra*] is not the right way!"

I will never forget the impact the Rav's reaction, even more than his words, made on me. Not only did he say not to leave out *any Pesukei D'zimra*, but he was very firm that saying them all *and* in their proper order is imperative. After that talk with Rav Auerbach, any day that I was running late I was very careful; I would go and daven at the later minyan so I could get all *Pesukei D'zimra* in order, just as the Rav had admonished me.

Last Tuesday morning I went to shul at Kehilat Bnei Torah's 6:25 minyan; I wanted very much to daven there. However, when I walked in it was already 6:30 — I was late by just five minutes. I realized that the only way to daven with my regular minyan was to either miss part of *Pesukei D'zimra* or to daven very, very fast in order to catch up with everyone else... neither of which I wanted to do. Rav Auerbach's admonition rang in my head. In those split seconds I thought of rushing my davening, and then immediately rejected the idea, telling myself, *"This is not the way to daven"* — and with that thought, though somewhat disappointed, I went upstairs. I would just have to wait for the upstairs 7:00 minyan in the main *beis medrash* instead. I settled myself in a chair and used the extra twenty minutes to learn.

At 6:50 I closed my *sefer* and began davening.

At 7:01 we suddenly heard a shout and then... shooting...

In shock and disbelief, instinct took over and we ran for our lives, tefillin on our heads, talleisim billowing out behind us. I dashed to the door of the main shul we were in, out the top side, fled up the outside stairs to Katzenellenbogen Street. Just as I got outside, I spotted another man jumping into his car. I jumped in as well and we sped off, toward the other side of Har Nof. We took refuge in Yeshivas Pachad Yitzchak, none of us believing what we had just heard. It took me a few seconds to catch my breath, but my first thought was of my own wife and children. I knew she would be up shortly, preparing them for school and sending them off. I did not want them to leave the house but when I called, no one answered. Then I remembered that my neighbor (Ansh) is certainly up then because I've seen her outside with her son many times, so I called her to ask her to inform my wife I was safe.

I feel that it is important to stress the magnitude of my personal *nes*: My regular seat in that minyan is on the *left-hand side of the beis medrash* near the front, where most of the casualties were. Nearly everyone who was butchered and hurt had been on the left-hand side of the shul because from that side you couldn't get out. Anyone on the left-hand side who did get out was an open miracle. I would have been sitting right there, together with or behind some of the others....

Later, when he got home, this man discovered that his alarm clock was mysteriously running four minutes slow, and it was apparently the cause of his fateful lateness that morning.

Several others among the 6:25 minyan regulars found themselves unable to attend that morning for a wide range of unexpected reasons. One *avreich* was woken up repeatedly in the night by his crying baby. Since he couldn't sleep, he decided, uncharacteristically, to go to *neitz* rather than wait for his regular minyan.

Meanwhile, Reb Meir Immanual was known for his "Yekkish" regularity in his attendance at the 6:25 Bnei Torah minyan for many years. Reb Meir is an older man who uses a walker, so he would catch a taxi every morning half a block away to arrive punctually at Bnei Torah. That Tuesday morning, to Reb Meir's consternation, his taxi did not show up as promised. It is awful to imagine how vulnerable he would have been if he had been at shul as usual.

Another older man, S.Z., lives directly across from Bnei Torah and planned to join the 6:25 a.m. minyan that Tuesday morning, as he had done every morning for some twenty years. However, he awoke that day with mysterious, excruciating aches in his legs. He felt obliged to stay at home instead. It should be noted that S.Z.'s regular place in shul was directly behind that of Rabbi Moshe Twersky, *Hy"d*, and he would have been in great peril if he had taken his usual place that morning.

One of the *gabbaim* of the shul planned to bring his son, whose bar mitzvah was a month away, to put on tefillin for the first time with the upstairs minyan. He invited some relatives to Bnei Torah to join this joyous occasion, including his brother-in-law, the renowned medical advocate Benny Fisher. However, since a family *simchah* ran very late the night before, the family decided to postpone the early-morning tefillin laying. As a result, no members of the family were at the shul as planned, and the boy's *simchah* did not end in trauma.

Rabbi Avraham Nadler, another prominent Har Nof rabbi, reported that he had davened in the 6:25 Bnei Torah minyan every day for over ten years. He switched to a nearby *neitz* minyan only shortly before that Tuesday morning, and was spared.

My own situation is similar. When I started to give a *shiur* at 6:30 a.m. in a different neighborhood, I reluctantly had to give up my regular place for weekday *Shacharis* at Bnei Torah.

During the Massacre

EVEN AMONG THOSE WHO WERE DESTINED to be at the 6:25 minyan, there emerged many stories of salvation that defy logic.

First and foremost, it is truly remarkable that more people were not hurt and killed, *chas veshalom*. The terrorists were in the shul for eleven minutes before the policemen arrived to take them on. They were armed with semi-automatic pistols and were targeting unarmed victims caught by surprise. They were young, strong and bent on devastation. If you read the minute-by-minute breakdown of the massacre at the start of this book, you may notice that the terrorists did not act efficiently and a lot of time was "wasted." Logically speaking, they should have been able to "accomplish" much more.

There can be no doubt that Hashem was there at that moment of darkness, orchestrating every movement of those involved. The terrorists were only able to do what Hashem willed them to do, no more and no less.

As the first group fled through this side door, the terrorists opened fire on them, but no one was hurt. Afterwards, the bullet holes were found in that area, including one lodged in the *aron kodesh*.

At one point, one of the terrorists encountered Rabbi B., who was coming down the stairs from the upstairs *beis medrash*, and rushed over to check on Rabbi Levine's lifeless body. The terrorist raised his weapon to shoot Rabbi B. point blank. He pulled the trigger at least four times, but for some reason the pistol jammed and no bullets emerged. Meanwhile, Rabbi B. was able to flee upstairs.

Another congregant had a similar experience, when one of the terrorists took point-blank aim at his head. The man heard the sound of the trigger being pulled, but then nothing happened. The gun was jammed. While the terrorist tried to fix it, the man fled to safety.

As noted earlier, one of the *kedoshim*, Rabbi Aryeh Kupinsky, confronted the terrorists and called for everyone else to "run" as he struggled with them. This distraction was very significant, since during the struggle more people fled the shul. During the Kupinsky *shivah*, several of the survivors told his family that they owed Rabbi Kupinsky their lives.

Incidentally, one of the survivors also felt that Rabbi Levine had saved many lives through his death, and told this to his widow at the *shivah*. Everyone inside the shul heard the fatal gunshots before the terrorists entered the *beis medrash* where they were *davening Shemoneh Esrei*. As a result, quite a few of the congregants were able to flee even before the terrorists came in, while the rest took cover as best as they could.

After the first terrorist's pistol jammed, the second terrorist began to attack the congregants with a meat cleaver. One of the men he struck several times was Rabbi Shmuel Goldstein. Despite his serious injuries, Rabbi Goldstein somehow found the strength to pull the terrorist to the ground. Several more congregants were able to flee during the scuffle. The second terrorist came over to Rabbi Goldstein, but instead of finishing him off, he merely yelled at him in Hebrew: "Get out of here!"

Rabbi Goldstein did get up and ran out of the shul on his own two feet. Once outside, he encountered Josh White, a former *talmid* of Yeshivas Machon Shlomo, who happened to be riding his bike down Agassi Street when he noticed the commotion. Josh immediately ripped off his shirt and used it to bandage Rabbi Goldstein's head.

Soon after, paramedics began arriving and Rabbi Goldstein was the first victim to receive medical treatment. The fact that the terrorist bizarrely let Rabbi Goldstein walk out of the shul in that way, at that time, may have saved his life, as he was able to get immediate treatment for his serious head wounds and stem the loss of blood.

Earlier, Rabbi Goldstein's 12-year-old son was able to flee the scene by crawling right between the legs of the two terrorists.

Two congregants positioned on the right side of the shul saw one of the terrorists coming toward them. One of them picked up a large table, and somehow found the strength to hurl it at their assailant. They then fled through the side door. The terrorist tried to pursue them, but was blocked by the overturned table.

Every person who was fated to be in that minyan, yet survived, came away with a sense of awe at the Hand of Hashem. Rabbi Chaim Ozer Sternbuch was among them, and he made a *seudas hodaah*, together with his father Rav Moshe Sternbuch, the Av Beis Din of Yerushalayim, the following Motzaei Shabbos.

As Rabbi Goldstein recalled later, while recovering in the hospital from his injuries:

"The first thing I said when I woke up was the *passuk* 'Ashirah laHashem bechayai,* I will sing to Hashem with my life.' Now I appreciate that so much more; that every second that Hashem gives me life, it's not a one-time present, it's a constant present that Hashem gives and keeps giving. I recognize all of the miracles that Hashem did in this story.

"Even though it is looked at as a very bad story, there are so many miracles that Hashem did; it could have been much worse."

Overcoming the Terrorists THE TERRORISTS MADE SOME BIZARRE tactical mistakes that allowed them to be quickly taken down by two policemen, even the though the latter were ill-prepared and poorly-equipped for the shootout.

Had the terrorists holed themselves up deep in the shul, they would have had the strategic advantage over anyone who tried to storm the building, and it would have taken much longer and much more police manpower to dislodge them.

However, after the police arrived and opened fire on

them, the terrorists decided to try to flee through the front door. Thus, they were easily gunned down at the entrance to the building.

The terrorists' decision to run for their lives in such a hopeless manner is very puzzling, but it appears that they imagined they could flee the scene. Such terrorists generally have a zero percent chance of remaining alive and usually take the attitude that they should do as much damage as they can while they are still alive, with total disregard for their own survival. In fact, they welcome the idea of dying on such a mission.

The strange actions of the terrorists saved Jewish lives, as the congregants still inside the shul and the police forces who were on their way to rescue them, would all have been in grave danger if they had acted more rationally.

The first outsiders to rush to the scene were two paramedics, Akiva Pollack and Yanky Ehrlich. Akiva Pollack later recounted that he happened to be only 400 meters away from Bnei Torah when he received the alert and was able to reach the shul in under a minute. He found Rabbi Goldstein bleeding and bandaged with a shirt outside. Rabbi Goldstein tried to tell him there was shooting inside, but since he was barely conscious and his injuries indicated stabbing, not shooting, Pollack and Ehrlich ventured into the building, unaware of what awaited them.

> "I walked into the lobby of the shul and saw a body lying on the floor, about 10 to 12 meters [32 to 39 feet] from the entrance," Akiva Pollack later said [referring to Kalman Levine]. "I dragged him out, and I'm on the phone with the dispatcher saying, 'It looks like a real serious scene going on here.' I guess the two terrorists inside heard me."

At that point, the two attackers started shooting at the paramedics, and they jumped down the steps to try to get more cover.

"I didn't have time to think," he said. "I just heard shooting coming toward me and I took off like the wind.

"[The other] paramedic slipped and cracked his ankle. Then I heard a scream; I thought he was shot. I saw bullets flying over his head."

But the attackers missed both paramedics with their shots, and Pollack was not injured. At that moment, the two policemen arrived, and the shootout began.

"I went to visit [Kalman Levine's] family when they were sitting *shivah*, and I told them with his death, he saved another three people from being killed — myself and two other Magen David Adom team members," Pollack said. "If we would have gone inside, we would have been shot."*

Police began to arrive in waves, but the first on the scene were two traffic cops, Zidan Seif and Itzik Weitzman. Both took cover at the entrance of the building and launched a gun battle with terrorists. The Druze policeman Seif was the first to open fire. Before doing so, he pushed a policewoman out of the way, probably saving her life. He was shot down and died of his wounds at Shaarei Zedek Hospital later that night.

Weitzman continued to engage the terrorists while more reinforcements arrived. As the two terrorists tried to flee the building, they were shot dead by a third police officer. Weitzman said afterwards that it was miraculous that the

---

* Excerpted from an interview given to the *Cleveland Jewish News.*

terrorists identified themselves so clearly and thus the police were able to target them properly. The entire incident was over in minutes and, amid the chaos and confusion, there was a significant risk that he would not be able to distinguish between the terrorists and the victims. For example, if one of the congregants had tried to flee at that moment, they could have accidently harmed him.

Regarding the policemen who took down the terrorists, there is much about their story that is remarkable. First of all, there is the fact that they happened to come when they did. Apart from them, it was over eleven minutes before any police arrived at the scene. Second, it is miraculous that they did their job so courageously and effectively, especially since none of them were trained or equipped to deal with an incident such as this.

The first two officers, Seif and Weitzman, were traffic cops. They wore no protective gear and were lightly armed. The third officer, who ultimately killed the terrorists, worked in a forensic lab and was unused to active service. He later related that he was driving to work on the Begin Expressway when he heard an alert for Har Nof. If you are familiar with Jerusalem's roads, you will know that Begin is about a ten-minute drive from Har Nof. This policeman could easily have ignored the call, since he was far away and this was not his job. Instead, he decided to drive over there and see if he could help, thus saving lives.

Following the Attack NEWS OF THE ATTACK AT FIRST SPREAD AS rumors within Har Nof, neighbor to neighbor, phone to phone. For some time, residents were instructed to stay in their homes, for fear that more terrorists could be on the loose.

The streets were eerily empty of all but paramedics and police; the only sound to be heard was the wails of countless sirens.

Soon the media began to arrive and reports of the attack spread across the city, the country and the world like wildfire.

Each of us can remember what we felt the moment we heard about it: shock, disbelief, horror, pain. Before any details were known, Jews across the globe opened their Books of *Tehillim* and began to pray for mercy for all involved.

Har Nof residents frantically called all their loved ones to verify that they were out of harm's way. For those who knew that their family members were likely in or around the Bnei Torah building, time stopped as they desperately tried to locate them. As one woman put it: "I was awoken by the sound of the phone ringing. It was my son. He said: 'Mom, don't worry. I'm okay.' That's when I knew something terrible must have happened."

Husbands called their wives, sons called their mothers, neighbors reassured one another, and everywhere people thanked Hashem that their loved ones were physically unscathed. But for a few Har Nof residents, no such reassurance came. They could not find answers about the fate of their husbands and fathers. No one knew. With each passing moment, it became more and more worrying that they had not heard from them.

Surely, he would have found a way by then to let us know that he's okay? But to contemplate the alternative was not an option.

Rebbetzin Tziporah Heller described how this situation

affected her own daughter, Miri, whose husband, Rabbi Shmuel Goldstein, was among the missing.

> By 7:20 we both realized that if she didn't hear from Shmuli, something was very wrong. The police and other services had no information as yet to give to the public, but a family friend who had seen the terror with his own eyes, said that Shmuli had been taken to Hadassah Ein Kerem.
>
> Then she got the call that you never want to get. The social worker said: "Come to Hadassah Ein Kerem. And don't come alone."

Sadly, four Har Nof families got even worse phone calls. In the hours following, the Jewish people absorbed the news that four men had died *al kiddush Hashem* in the massacre.

> Rabbi Avrohom Shmuel Goldberg, 68.
>
> Rabbi Aryeh Kupinsky, 43.
>
> Rabbi Kalman Ze'ev Levine, 55.
>
> Rabbi Moshe Twersky, 59.

All of them were husbands and fathers. All of them were residents of Agassi Street. All of them were English-speaking immigrants; three from the United States, one from England.

The news of the Har Nof Massacre shocked Jews throughout Israel and all over the world deeply. It seemed inconceivable that at this point in history, Jews could be cut down so brutally while immersed in prayer.

"I don't ever remember seeing a disaster scene as shocking," said ZAKA founder Yehudah Meshi-Zahav, a veteran of countless scenes of terror. "The victims were wrapped in tallis and tefillin, pools of blood, siddurim all over the floor. A scene only recognized in the Holocaust. Those were Jews who got up early in the morning to pray to the Creator of the world. And in the midst of that, of peace and not conflict, they were attacked. I have never seen anything like this although I have seen terror attacks. It is the type of thing that enters your head and you can't forget…"

News outlets published graphic images: holy books soaked with blood and pocked with bullet holes; tefillin wrapped around a lifeless arm. These images arouse a deep and primal Jewish memory inside our people.

Many people said they should not have been published at all. That they were too traumatic, too difficult to erase from memory, disrespectful to the *niftarim* and their families.

News is news, and most media outlets do not resist the temptation to attract a larger audience through sensationalism. But that is not the purpose of this book. We deliberately decided not to include any photos because we want to keep our attention on the inside story and deeper message.

In truth, most of us don't need photos to relate to the story. Many people across the Torah world are familiar with Har Nof, which is home to many yeshivahs, seminaries and thousands of English-speaking families. No one could comprehend that such a scene had taken place that very day in the familiar hillside suburb, a quiet neighborhood generally removed from the bustle of the city.

But by that afternoon, all four *kedoshim* had been laid to rest, with the *Kaddish* recited by twenty-four fresh orphans before thousands of mourners. Three of the *levayos* were held together on Agassi Street, right outside Kehilat Bnei Torah. Rabbi Twersky's *levayah* was held in the neighborhood of

Sanhedria HaMurchevet at Yeshivas Toras Moshe, where he was a rebbi for over twenty years.

Then the four families sat down for four separate Agassi Street *shivahs*.

Meanwhile, the Jewish people around the world continued to pray for the recovery of the injured being treated in Jerusalem's hospitals. Several were fighting for their lives. We groped our way through the darkness of grim questions:

How did this happen?

Why did this happen?

What should we do now?

Insights coming from the great leaders and teachers of our generation are collected later in this book. They seek the message in this inconceivable tragedy, so that we might understand Hashem's ways a little better.

An Outpouring of Love

THE HAR NOF MASSACRE ALSO UNLEASHED an unprecedented outpouring of *chessed* and Jewish unity. Jews from across Israel and around the world sought ways to show comfort and caring for the victims' families.

Literally millions of dollars were raised for their relief within the space of a week. Many of the fundraising efforts were grassroots. Fundraising efforts were initiated by the local Tomchei Shabbos charity fund and Kupat Ha'Ir. This was augmented by the impromptu Help Har Nof fund, launched by concerned Jews in New York. Together they raised an incredible $2.4 million from caring donors around the world, within just ten days. About $1.1 million of that came as matching funds from a few anonymous benefactors, thanks to the efforts of Rabbi Nissan Kaplan, a prominent Har Nof rabbi and member of the Bnei Torah community. The rest of the donations flooded in organically from thousands of donors. There was no advertising campaign or incentive to donate. News of the fund spread entirely by word of mouth — a testimony to how many people were touched by the Har Nof Massacre and inspired to show their caring for the victims.

Meanwhile, trucks from the Rami Levi supermarket chain arrived at the homes of the four *kedoshim*, as well as the home of the Druze police officer's family, and unloaded many boxes of food and candy, along with an envelope of supermarket vouchers. On it was written, "Rami Levi shares in your pain."

The most severely wounded of the survivors was Chaim Yechiel ben Malka (Rothman). Chaim moved to Israel from Toronto, Canada, more than thirty years ago, but the passage of years did not diminish the caring of former neighbors, classmates and the wider Toronto Jewish community. Holding a *Tehillim* rally for his *refuah sheleimah*, they expressed faith that he would recover, with G-d's help, but also concern that his rehabilitation would be drawn out and that he may not be able to return to work and support his wife and ten children. Within days, the UJA Federation of Greater Toronto set up the Howie Rothman & Family Victim of Terror Assistance Fund, to assist the Rothman family financially through the short- and long-term challenges that they face.

Beyond the financial assistance that thousands of donors felt moved to offer and the mass *Tehillim* groups and countless prayers, some people got creative in their efforts to show their caring from a distance.

For example, the Friday after the *shivah*, the bereaved families were surprised when a large bouquet of Shabbos flowers was delivered to their doors, courtesy of the members of Thornhill Woods Shul in Toronto, Canada. The shul has arranged that each of the bereaved families and some of the families of the injured will have fresh flowers delivered to their homes every *erev Shabbos* for the next four months.

The daughter of one of the *kedoshim* wrote to thank them:

Today we *were* and *weren't* surprised by the beautiful flowers that came to our door!

We *were* surprised because we weren't expecting to receive a beautiful bunch of flowers from our wonderful brethren so many thousands of miles away.

We *weren't* surprised because we know that when one part of *Klal Yisrael* is in pain we all feel it.

The flowers are in a beautiful vase and are adorning our dining room for Shabbos. When we look at them, we will remember how much *Klal Yisrael* cares about us and all those in pain.

A few days after the massacre, many Har Nof residents heard a knock at their door. On their doorsteps they found some teenage girls, who handed them a pre-packaged cake and a printed note that read as follows:

We are going through some difficult days.
We are dealing with a reality that is not simple and is scary.
We, the students of the Even Shmuel Girls' High School in the south of Israel, feel a part of you at this difficult time.
We came to tell you that you are not alone in the face of terrorism in Israel. We stand with Jerusalem.
The Jewish people care for you and stand by you.
The eternal people do not fear the long road.

The note, decorated with hearts, was brought all the way from the south of Israel, which has suffered so much at the hands of terrorists recently.

One week after the massacre, hundreds of Har Nof families got another sweet surprise — a block of *kosher l'mehadrin* chocolate delivered by a group of unknown teenage boys. Even sweeter was the note that accompanied the gift. It read as follows:

> To our dear brothers and sisters, the residents of Har Nof!
>
> The Jewish people are one body and one soul. The pain is nationwide. All of Israel is deeply in pain.
>
> In our most difficult time, many Jews stood by our side. And now, we are at your side…
>
> With love,
The residents of Itamar

Itamar is the settlement near Shechem in the Shomron that suffered the horrific massacre of the Fogel family in 2011.

These gestures seem small, or merely cute, but they are important because they recognize the fact that while only a few families were overtly impacted by the massacre, the entire neighborhood of Har Nof was traumatized by it. Feelings of fear and helplessness can be eased by shows of understanding and compassion. Even small gestures like this can mean a lot.

Meanwhile, the community of Har Nof is doing its best to move on. Even the very next day, the sounds of Torah learning and davening filled that same *beis medrash*, with the bullet holes still in the *sefarim* and *aron kodesh*.

One of the survivors, Dr. Yitzchak (Norm) Heching returned to Bnei Torah the next day, and told the media: "They are not going to stop me from doing what I need to do: living in Israel, praying in Israel, leading a normal life. They are not going to stop me."

The people of Har Nof move on, but they are not unchanged by this massacre.

In Gratitude THE COMMUNITY ALSO FELT IT IMPORTANT TO express its gratitude to Zidan Seif, the 30-year-old Druze policeman killed while bravely trying to stop the terrorists, and extend support to his family. Rav Rubin, the Rav of Kehilat Bnei Torah, traveled to Seif's home village in northern Israel to deliver a eulogy at the funeral.

"We came from Jerusalem, from the place of the massacre... simply to be with you and to cry with you," he told the mourners. "Zidan showed courage. He was the first at the battle. He stood like a wall, with his body, with his head, in order to save the souls of those in the synagogue. The loss of Zidan is our loss as well as that of the Druze community and we feel, especially at times like this, a kinship with the Druze community. The devotion and the determination of Zidan should be an example to us all — to the Druze and to the Jews."

One Har Nof resident chartered buses so that dozens of people could attend the funeral and represent the gratitude and condolences of the community.

A week after the massacre, the Har Nof community invited Seif's parents, widow, relatives and friends to Kehilat Bnei Torah to thank them personally for his sacrifice. Survivors and family members welcomed them and showed them where their son gave his life to save the surviving Jews in the shul from further harm by the terrorists.

"You know in our religion we are proud of everyone who sacrifices themselves to save others. You'll go above [to Heaven] and you'll be proud of him, he'll be in a place of honor," one thankful congregant told Seif's father. "Someone who saves lives, he receives… With G-d's help, may you have only joy and pride. And it's not just him, it's your education, the education of all the family that caused him to do it."

The community also offered to set up a fund to help support Seif's young widow and baby daughter. At first Seif's family refused, but after the meeting at Bnei Torah, they accepted a renewed offer. Immediately, a call was issued to raise money for the Seif family. In response, a fundraising campaign was launched by a group of tenth graders at Rambam Mesivta in Lawrence, New York, with the goal of raising $100,000 for the widow and orphan.

A righteous gentile who had the *zechus* to save Jewish lives deserves to be honored always.

The Story and the Truth   THE HAR NOF MASSACRE CAUSED A TREMENDOUS loss of four beloved Jews, who seemingly still had so much to offer this world. It led to immeasurable mental and physical suffering for the injured and their families. It traumatized countless people to various degrees — even those who were far away from the scene, were filled with fear and helplessness.

The road to recovery is long.

There is no way to deny or avoid the excruciating pain of it.

But there is also no denying that Hashem's Hand is

clearly visible in this story, if we resist the urge to turn our faces away, and instead heed the call to view it through the eyes of *emunah*.

Rebbetzin Chaya Levine, widow of Rabbi Kalman Levine, showed us the way when she declared at the *shivah*:

"Arabs did not kill my husband! He was taken as a *korban* by the *Borei Olam*!"

MEMORIES

*"It is a sign of both his gadlus and his anivus that
we have learned more about his maasim tovim
in the weeks since his passing than
we knew in his lifetime."*

– Rabbi Meir Salasnik, shlita

RABBI AVROHOM SHMUEL GOLDBERG HY"D
The Nine-Hour *Baal Habayis*

By Rabbi Daniel Yaakov Travis, shlita

Achieving Synthesis THE RAMBAM WROTE, "IF A PERSON IS A *BAAL habayis* — for example, he works three hours a day and learns nine hours..." (*Hilchos Talmud Torah* 1:12). My Rosh Yeshivah, Harav Tzvi Kushelevsky, once said that when he goes abroad to collect, he strives to maintain at least the level of the *baal habayis* of the Rambam, learning nine hours each day. In our generation it is extremely rare to find a working person who works three hours and learns nine hours. Why is it that in the times of the Rambam it was possible, while today it is so difficult? During my years in yeshivah and *kollel* I was always bothered by this question.

Until I became a *Rosh Kollel.* In my new life-circumstances, I had to go running around in *chutz la'aretz* trying to raise funds so that my *talmidim* would have food to eat. I saw firsthand that under such circumstances, when one is so busy and pulled into the chaos of modern-day life, even setting aside a small amount of time to be able to learn and to daven properly is a great *nisayon.* Anyone who can learn more than that — and certainly someone who learns nine hours a day — demonstrates the attribute of *gevurah,* the greatest strength to overcome the hustle and bustle of everyday life.

I do not know if Rabbi Avrohom Shmuel Goldberg learned nine hours a day, but one thing I do know: Whenever I entered the *beis medrash* of Kehilat Bnei Torah and saw him, he was either davening or learning. He spent the entire morning learning in the *beis medrash* with his *chavrusa*. For a long time I was not sure if he was an *avreich* or a *baal habayis*. Even after I learned that he worked, I believe it would have been more accurate to call him a *baal habayis* in the Rambam's sense.

Walking Softly HOW DOES ONE REACH THE LEVEL AT WHICH HE can be a "Rambam-*baal habayis*" in today's society, which literally pulls one away from Torah and *tefillah*? The answer depends on what a person's level of devotion to Torah was before he started to work. If he was fully dedicated to Torah while in yeshivah, as Rabbi Goldberg was during his years of study in Gateshead, then that dedication will remain with him even when he enters the workplace.

A fellow *talmid* in Gateshead Yeshivah related that when he himself was learning in Gateshead he had felt that on some level of his identity he was not just Jewish but also an Englishman, while Rav Avrohom Shmuel was "Jewish through and through." When Rav Avrohom Shmuel left yeshivah to pursue a degree, the *rabbanim* made sure to tell him that he was always welcome back. A few years later he did return, and received *semichah* from the Rosh Yeshivah, a *semichah* that almost no one (including many of his closest relatives) even knew he had. This connection to the yeshivah continued, and on various occasions, in his quiet, humble manner, he helped out the yeshivah in many ways.

A Deep Sense of Respect AT THE *LEVAYAH*, HIS SON-IN-LAW RAV Binyomin Hammond, a *maggid shiur* in the Mir Yeshivah, delivered a *hesped* on his father-in-law. Rav Hammond relayed that his father-in-law loved *rabbanim* and *sefarim*. He personified the words of the *passuk*, "Torah is a Tree of Life for those who cling to it."

One of the *rebbeim* in Yeshivas Mir related that as a young *avreich* he was speaking to someone during *Lecha Dodi,* and Rabbi Goldberg came over to him and said calmly, "How can one speak during davening?" Similarly, *mispallelim* in the minyan where he davened related how he was *makpid* on the decorum of the shul.

For many years I walked home from *Maariv* almost every night at the same time as Rabbi Goldberg, who lived next door to me. What struck me most about him was his regality. He was a person of stature, honor and dignity. It was clear to me that such refinement was possible only for someone who had worked on himself and shaped his life through Torah.

Rabbi Goldberg's speech matched the regality of the way he walked. He spoke so gently and kindly — I cannot even imagine him ever getting angry. Rav Avrohom Shmuel spoke in the way *Chazal* describe as the manner in which a Jew is meant to speak. Moreover, he personified what *Chazal* tell us: "Always greet others with a friendly countenance."

A Man of Caring RABBI GOLDBERG MANAGED TARGUM PRESS for a number of years. One of his employees, C.B. Gavant, relates, "In our close-knit Jerusalem office, with all *frum* staff, he wanted to get to know all of his employees, and this wasn't hard to do. The only hitch was that I was living overseas at the time. He made an effort to call me so we would become acquainted. That gesture told me that, despite the distance, I would be working for a boss who cared. When I returned to Israel a year later, Rabbi Goldberg again found time to meet with me to discuss the new terms of my employment and to make sure I felt comfortable in my new-old environment....

"At one point in my nearly three years working under him, I had to take an extended leave of absence, for personal reasons. Rabbi Goldberg accepted the situation with equanimity and gave me as much time as I needed, waiting until I felt better before inviting me to return."

An *avreich* who had done some translating work for Rabbi Goldberg related that they had arranged to meet in the *avreich's* yeshivah during night *seder*. Surprised that Rabbi Goldberg didn't show up, the *avreich* got up to leave; then he saw Rabbi Goldberg at the back of the *beis medrash*, waiting patiently for him to finish learning. "I didn't want to disturb your learning," Rabbi Goldberg told him.

One of the *menachamim* at the *shivah* related that a few weeks earlier he too had been sitting *shivah*, and Rabbi Goldberg had come to be *menachem* him. The visitors who were there before he arrived rose to leave, then just the two of them remained in the room. Rabbi Goldberg waited there with him for a long time until the next person came, so as not to leave the *avel* on his own.

Mispallelim in the 6:25 Kehilat Bnei Torah minyan describe how Rabbi Goldberg would arrive early and rearrange the chairs and the *shtenders*, so that the rest of the minyan would find the *beis medrash* ready for *tefillah*. For many years he sat next to Rav Twersky, and every morning he would set out the siddur that the Rav used for davening.

In our generation there is so much to do that on occasion we may not have time to treat others with the proper respect. Rabbi Goldberg viewed every Jew as a child of Avraham, Yitzchak and Yaakov, and the way he related to all of them was in line with this recognition. May we all learn from his beautiful ways of peace and try to shape our lives accordingly.

Memories of a Mensch

By Rabbi Meir Salasnik, shlita
Mara D'asra Bushey, England

A VROHOM SHMUEL GOLDBERG, WHO GREW UP IN LIVER-pool, England, came from a family of distinguished Rabbis and Jewish community leaders in the United Kingdom. He was the only child of Aharon (Harry) and Jessie Goldberg.

Jessie's father was Menachem Yehudah (Mendel) Sheinfeld, whose own father was a Rosh Yeshivah in a place called Reshain (possibly Rietavas) near Kovno. Coming to Britain as a young man in 1908, he served the Jewish community in various capacities in Bradford, then Manchester, and, in 1911, moved to Cardiff, Wales, where he was a chazzan, *shochet* and *mohel* for the following twenty-five years until his death at the age of 60 in 1936.

Aharon's father, Avrohom Shmuel Goldberg, after whom his grandson was named, died in 1940 at the age of 65. He lived in Liverpool, where he gave a regular *shiur* in cooperation with Rabbi Unterman, then the Rav of Liverpool, and later Chief Rabbi of Tel Aviv and Israel. Avrohom Shmuel the elder was also on the board of the Liverpool Yeshivah.

Rabbi Unterman's successor as community Rav of Liverpool was Rabbi Plitnick. Only recently, the younger Avrohom Shmuel donated a *Shas* to a *kollel* in memory of Rabbi Plitnick.

Descended from the Tosfos Yom Tov, Aharon himself was a *shochet* in Liverpool, where one of his brothers was a well-known doctor. Aharon Goldberg also died while davening *Shacharis* — in his case from natural causes. It is as if Hashem has emphasized the closeness this family has to *tefillah*. Avrohom Shmuel was always punctual for davening.

Although Avrohom Shmuel was an only child, as both parents came from large families, he had many cousins and kept strong connections with them throughout his life. His interest in family led him to compile and aid others in compiling family trees. Like everything he did, he accomplished this in a methodical and orderly fashion. Even the *"shanah tovah"* greeting he sent out by email was arranged in an orderly and tasteful format.

Citing the verse in *Tehillim* (97:11), *"Uleyishrei lev simchah"* — happiness for the upright of heart — Rabbi Gershon Hager of Golders Green, London, a friend and *chavrusa* of Avrohom Shmuel, recalled at the *hesped* he gave in London following the *shivah* that Avrohom Shmuel was always *b'simchah*. A smile never left his face.

Avrohom Shmuel shone both in school and at the Liverpool Yeshivah, from where he continued on to Sheffield University, where he studied chemical engineering, and Imperial College, London, where he specialized in powder technology and bulk solids. While in Sheffield University, he also went to Gateshead Yeshivah.

He organized the First International Powder Technology and Bulk Solids Conference in Harrogate, England, in 1971, when he was around 25 years old, and moderated the proceedings. He continued to organize conferences and publish in scientific publications for over twenty years.

One of his oldest friends from Liverpool, his relative Arnold Lewis, described him as "a kind, humble and generous person — a genuine mensch — whom I was privileged to count as a friend and with whom I had been corresponding regularly over many years. He was immensely knowledgeable and took a special interest in Liverpool Jewish communal history. He was also a keen 'mishpachologist.'"

Avrohom Shmuel left Liverpool nearly fifty years ago. However, the high esteem in which he and his family were held, as well as the shocking manner of his murder, was such that hundreds of people came to Childwall Shul in Liverpool on short notice for a memorial service.

I first met Avrohom Shmuel a little over forty years ago. He had briefly taken a position as secretary of Eitz Chaim Yeshiva in London and also gave an after-school Gemara *shiur* to a number of boys. A few years later, I married his wife's cousin.

During the last eight years, I have been an occasional visitor to Har Nof, as my son, daughter-in-law and grandchildren live there, close to the Boston Shul. There are many minyanim available to me daily within a five-minute walk. However, the opportunity to sit next to Avrohom Shmuel during *tefillah* was so worthwhile that on a few Shabbos and Yom Tov mornings, I climbed the mountain to Agassi Street. On one occasion, he pointed out to me a man sitting a couple of rows in front of him and said this was the grandson of the Tolner Rebbe and also a grandson of Rav Yosef Dov Soloveitchik [this was Rabbi Moshe Twersky, *Hy"d*]. I was taken aback that one who was both a descendant of Chassidish Rebbes and the Brisker dynasty was sitting at the back of shul, and then it occurred to me that this was part of his modesty. It was also part of Avrohom Shmuel's modesty that he sat at the back. Both of these modest men, with other *kedoshim*, entered *Olam Haba* together.

Part of Avrohom Shmuel's modesty was that very few people knew he had *semichah*. Even many in his close family were unaware of this.

I hope it is not too much of an exaggeration to cite the Gemara in *Sukkah* where we learn that Rabban Yochanan ben Zakkai was the least of Hillel's eighty star *talmidim*. Most of the other seventy-nine, while compared in greatness to either Moshe or Yehoshua, are anonymous to us — *gedolim* who chose the back seats!

Some twenty years ago, for the benefit of the *chinuch* of the family, the Goldbergs made aliyah, initially to Ofakim, where Avrohom Shmuel learned half a day and worked half a day, and then moved to Har Nof.

He was a *mokir rabbanan*. He supported many institutions, including the maintenance of Liverpool's Rice Lane Cemetery, where relatives were buried. A short while ago, he discussed with me the state of the *matzeivah* of one of his uncles in Bushey Cemetery, close to my own home.

He had a wide knowledge of *sefarim* and Judaica, and was an appropriate editor for a few years at Targum Press. He would comment to me about articles I wrote for the *Daf Hashavua* of the United Synagogue in London, occasionally drawing my attention to nuances that I had not noted.

It is a sign of both his *gadlus* and his *anivus* that we have learned more about his *maasim tovim* in the weeks since his passing than we knew in his lifetime.

A Pillar That Upheld the World*

By Rav Tzvi Kushelevsky, shlita
Rosh Yeshivas Heichal HaTorah

RABI YOSSI SAID, "MAY MY PORTION BE AMONG THOSE WHO die while performing a mitzvah" (*Shabbos* 118b). The Maharal (ibid.) explains that someone who engages in a mitzvah shows that he is distanced from the mundane and clings to *kedushah*. Rabi Yossi longed to die while performing a mitzvah because this would demonstrate the dedication to *ruchnius* that he displayed during his lifetime.

The Mishnah (*Avos* 1:2) tells us that the world stands on three pillars: Torah, *avodah* and *gemilus chassadim*. Rav Aryeh Kupinsky, *Hashem yinkom damo*, excelled in all three areas, but above all he had an almost otherworldly mastery of the *middah* of *chessed*. All of *Klal Yisrael* are praised for their distinguishing acts of kindness, but Rav Aryeh was unique. In order to gain perspective on Rav Aryeh's level of *chessed*, let us analyze various types of *chessed*.

There are different levels of *chessed*. Some will perform acts of kindness only when they feel it is expected of them — for example, they will help to clear the table after a meal

---

* This *hesped* was delivered on 8 Kislev at Yeshivas Heichal HaTorah, Har Nof. It was transcribed by Rabbi Chaim Burman and appeared in the American *Yated Ne'eman* on 12 Kislev 5775.

because etiquette demands it. Aryeh performed *chessed* because he loved to do *chessed*, not because it was the polite thing to do. Indeed, when the Kupinsky family was invited out for a Shabbos meal, Aryeh would help to clean up. But a *chessed* done because of etiquette is a lower level of *chessed*.

Some go a step further and will help people in need even when no one expects their assistance. Before Pesach, Aryeh was part of a matzah-baking *chaburah*. After the arduous work of banging and kneading the dough, whoever finished their duties would step out, exhausted, to rest. Aryeh would stay behind and assist those in the *chaburah* who were still struggling to complete their task. This is the next level of *chessed*; when a chance for kindness presents itself, it is to be seized.

Aryeh went further, however. He would seek opportunities to do *chessed*; it didn't have to be public. He longed for the chance to help others. He ran a *gemach* for freezers, which he personally would deliver to those who needed them. This meant lugging heavy freezers around the steep roads and buildings of Har Nof, and people would ask him, "Aryeh, why do you do this strenuous work?" Their questions surprised him; he couldn't understand their reluctance to assist, even under these difficult circumstances.

This is the next level of *chessed* — when it begins to impinge on our own comfort. Some will perform acts of kindness until it reaches the point that it is no longer "good" for them. Others will persist even when it becomes inconvenient and difficult, ensuring that the other's needs are met. A man in Har Nof has *yahrtzeit* on Motzaei Yom Kippur, and since he cannot daven from the *amud* in shul, he needs to gather a minyan at his home. Aryeh was always there, before breaking his fast, to make up the minyan.

Yet another level of *chessed* is that which causes pain or distress to the one who performs it. Tragically, two years ago Aryeh's fourteen-year-old daughter passed away in her sleep. Every Rosh Chodesh Adar Aryeh would put on a costume hat and would help children cross the road and distribute sweets. Even after the *petirah* of his dear daughter, despite his pain, Aryeh kept up this practice. Although it brought back vivid memories of his daughter, he continued to bring *simchah* to children in Adar.

In the midst of his pain, he would dedicate himself to the needs of others. About a year ago, the father of one of our *talmidim* from Los Angeles was *niftar* and was brought to Eretz Yisrael for *kevurah*, which was to be on Har Hazeisim on a Friday afternoon. Aryeh accompanied the *levayah* and wept through it. When asked why he was in such pain, he responded that the *levayah* brought back the experience of his own daughter's *petirah*, and he was reliving the experience.

The *levayah* had been delayed, and the *chevrah kaddisha* began to murmur that there was not enough time, and the *kevurah* would have to take place on Motzaei Shabbos. It had already been quite some time since the *petirah*, however, and the family was anxious to perform the *kevurah* as soon as possible; so they moved forward quickly with the *levayah*. But when they reached the grave it became obvious that there was barely enough space prepared for the *niftar*, and the *chevrah kaddisha* pronounced that there was no time to widen the *kever* and the *levayah* would have to recommence on Motzaei Shabbos. In the midst of his pain Aryeh immediately stepped forward, raised the *mittah* and gently lowered it into the *kever*, fitting it in perfectly!

The ultimate level of *chessed* is to sacrifice one's life for the good of others — that person's portion is among those who die while performing a mitzvah. Aryeh lived a life of *chessed*, and would ultimately die performing the highest *chessed*. Let me describe what happened on that bitter morning: The barbaric murderers entered the shul during *Shacharis*, brandishing knives and an axe. They sought to wreak destruction on anyone they could attack, starting with the old and infirm, the most indefensible. The *mispallelim* dashed for the exit — "*Chayecha kodmim*" — one's own life takes precedence, but not Aryeh…

The Gemara at the end of *Maseches Yevamos* (122b) recounts a story: A man came before Rabi Tarfon to testify for an *agunah* that her husband had indeed been killed. He related the following:

"He and I were traveling together," he said, "when a band of rouges began to chase after us. He [the *almanah's* husband] pulled off a branch from a nearby tree and warded off the attackers.

"'*Aryeh* — lion!' I exclaimed to him. '*Aryeh*! *Yeyasher kochacha*!'

"He responded, 'That's right! Where I come from they call me Yochanan ben Yonasan "*Aryeh*" ["the lion"].'

"Not long afterwards, he said, '*yeyasher kochacha*!'… and then '*Aryeh*' died."

Aryeh Kupinsky, in his final act of kindness, the apex of *chessed*, personified the attribute of a lion. With a *lev aryeh* he was murdered *al kiddush Hashem*. Upon seeing the murderers enter the shul, though he had no weapon, he didn't flee; he began to throw tables and *shtenders* at the murderers to buy time so that others could escape. In the midst of that final *chessed*, Rav Aryeh was brutally murdered. He had such a level of

chessed, of *kedushah*, and that came from his *lev aryeh* —
a heart that was so completely committed to doing kindness
for others, that he would give his life in a final heroic act of
chessed.

This was the *middah* of *chessed* that Aryeh embodied!
Nevertheless, he personified all the pillars on which the
world stands. He would learn Torah with *mesirus nefesh*, ex-
erting himself in *sugyos* and *masechtos* — and he knew them.
One could name any *sugya* that he had learned and he could
repeat its contents clearly in sequence. He reached great
depths of understanding in his learning; he was a person who
lived his Torah.

He also excelled in the pillar of *avodah*. On the *passuk*
(*Devarim* 11:13), "You shall serve the Lord your G-d with all
your heart," *Chazal* teach (*Taanis* 2a) that the "service of the
heart" is *tefillah*. Aryeh would daven as if he were standing
before the *Kisei Hakavod*, before the *Shechinah*. He exemplified the words of Rabbeinu Yonah that one who davens can
be released from the physical world and his *neshamah* can be
freed from the confines of the body.

Everyone has been asking, "Why was it specifically the
tzaddikim who were the victims of this tragedy? What does
Hashem want from us?" The Gemara states (*Bava Kama* 60a)
that when a Divine decree of punishment is to be delivered,
the tzaddikim are first removed from the world. Rashi explains that this is to save them from the distress of witnessing
the coming destruction. What is happening now is a wake-up
call from *Shamayim*; we are experiencing a warning of something much worse that could follow. We need to consider
why this could be, and what we can do to prevent it.

It is true that the enemies of Torah are attempting to

uproot Torah study. However, blaming a cause outside ourselves for the attempted destruction of our yeshivos is to miss the message Hashem is trying to relay to us, the *bnei Torah*. He wants to show us what needs to be rectified.

The Bach (*Hilchos Chanukah, Orach Chaim* 670) states that the reason the Yevanim were able to prohibit the Jews' practice of their *avodos* was that the Jews themselves had become lazy and indolent in their *avodah*. When our Torah study is weak and we do not maximize our potential, it invites harsh judgment from *Shamayim*. The terrible events of recent times are a call to renew our commitment to Torah study, to strengthen our allegiance to Torah.

When Hashem takes tzaddikim from this world, it is as if *Klal Yisrael* has offered a *korban*. There are two conditions needed for a *korban* (*Vayikra* 22:21): It must be pure (*tamim*) and must be offered willingly (*l'ratzon*). Aryeh's death was a pure *korban* to Hashem, and I have no doubt that had he been asked if he would be willing for what happened to transpire, he would have answered in the affirmative; so was his character. He was taken because of our shortfalls, a *korban* for our transgressions.

But how could we possibly console the *almanah*? This I can tell you: The Father of *yesomim* and Protector of *almanos*, He shall protect and guard you. Aryeh was taken as a pure *korban*, pure in his *middos*, pure in his attributes and pure in his Torah. Hashem will help you, Hashem will help: "And Hashem shall wipe away the tears from all faces" (*Yeshayah* 25:8), *v'nomar amen*.

RABBI ARYEH KUPINSKY *HY"D*

Chessed without Limits*

By Rabbi Daniel Yaakov Travis, shlita

The Punishment Fits the Crime
ON SHABBOS, JUST A FEW DAYS BEFORE Rav Aryeh was murdered, he and I had spoken in learning, as we always did after the *neitz* minyan. In the course of the conversation, for some reason he brought up *yom hamisah*, the day of death, and I was a bit shocked. Little did I know that Hashem was preparing me for a much greater shock. Aryeh! If I had known this was the last time we would ever speak, I would have hugged and kissed you!

"The punishment fits the crime," people often say. Hashem punished us with great fury by taking from among us Aryeh and the other *kedoshim*. How could He take a father just two years after taking this man's daughter! If He could punish us with such fury, He must be demanding of us something huge.

For four years I was *zocheh* to learn in the *shiur* of our Rosh Yeshivah, Hagaon Harav Tzvi Kushelevsky, *shlita*. During that time I gained a tremendous amount, but perhaps the most important thing I learned is not to be *"shidchi"* —

---

* This *hesped* was delivered on 8 Kislev at Yeshivas Heichal HaTorah, Har Nof. It appeared in the American *Yated Ne'eman* on 12 Kislev 5775.

superficial. Indeed, we must be *maamik* — we must delve deeply into the *sugya* of Rav Aryeh's death and try to understand what it is that Hashem wants from us.

Open-House Policy
ALTHOUGH RAV ARYEH EXCELLED IN TORAH and *tefillah*, his *gadlus* was in *chessed*. When we think of the great efforts Rav Aryeh made to do *chessed*, thinking constantly about what other people need, we are astounded. How can someone do so much *chessed*?

But this is not even a question. Rav Aryeh is actually the norm, the way a Jew is meant to be: *rodef chessed* — pursuing opportunities to do *chessed* without limit. The fact that such questions enter our minds shows that we all have much to improve in order to become what a Jew is meant to be. *Chazal* tell us that the right question to ask is, "When will my actions reach the level of the *Avos*, Avraham, Yitzchak and Yaakov?"

We are all willing to do *chessed* when a need comes along. If we help out a bit, we feel that we have fulfilled our obligation of *chessed*. Not Rav Aryeh. He never felt that he had fulfilled his obligation. Just the opposite. He was always looking for new opportunities.

We can learn the *middah* of *chessed* without limit from the *Avos* and *Imahos*. Everyone knows that Avraham Avinu's tent had four doors, so that he could usher in guests from all sides. When we first hear this it sounds like a beautiful thing, but there is so much more to it. Avraham Avinu was teaching us about the true nature of *chessed* for which a Jew is meant to strive.

A door facing each direction shows that a person wants

to destroy all the walls and make his home open to the entire world; that he wants to be able to give to everyone, with no limitations; that he has walls on his house only to protect him from the elements. Four doors is the closest one can come to a true "open-house policy" and still have a home.

An Appropriate Shidduch

WHEN IT CAME TIME FOR AVRAHAM Avinu to look for a *shidduch* for Yitzchak, he sent his faithful *talmid* Eliezer. Eliezer asked Hashem to send him a girl who would draw water for him and also for all of his camels. This was a bizarre test, considering that Rivka was only three years old and Eliezer had ten strong servants to help him.

Eliezer wanted to make sure that Yitzchak's future wife would have the same *middah* as Avraham Avinu. The *rodef chessed* does not feel satisfied unless he has done every *chessed* he is capable of doing. Eliezer tested Rivka in this way to make sure that she possessed a burning drive to do *chessed* without limits.

The root of the *middah* of *chessed* is *bitul atzmius* — eliminating all selfishness from one's life. Dovid Hamelech, who achieved this level, described it beautifully when he wrote (*Tehillim* 142:8), "Remove my soul from the fetters of my *self* to thank Your Name ... because You have given to me." When a person breaks down the barriers erected by his *self*, then he can think clearly and thank Hashem, and he can be a real giver to others.

Rav Aryeh was a complete giver. There was no such word as *selfish* in Rav Aryeh's vocabulary. He woke up every morning and went to sleep every night with one thought in mind: *How can I give to others without limit?*

Rav Aryeh's roommate in yeshivah said that Rav Aryeh had a sign over his bed stating, "Whatever you want, please take without asking." He personified what *Chazal* tell us: "What's yours is yours and what's mine is yours." We must make every effort to fill the void left in the world with Rav Aryeh's passing and try to practice the attribute of *chessed* without limits.

A Timely Gemach

SOME PEOPLE WOULD SINK INTO DEPRESSION IF their fourteen-year-old daughter passed away; not Aryeh. This tragedy only spurred him to do more and more *chessed*. He told me excitedly about his ideas, handing out candies to all the children of the neighborhood on Rosh Chodesh Adar, sponsoring *shiurim* and *sefarim*, and even running a freezer *gemach*.

Rav Aryeh told me why he started this *gemach*: People need to make a *kiddush*; catering these events is expensive — most people cannot afford catering. The solution is to bake a lot of cakes in advance; but then where do you store all that cake?

There are many types of *gemachim* among *Klal Yisrael* — money, chairs, even pacifiers, but as far as I know, nowhere in the world is there another *gemach* for freezers that are delivered by the head of the *gemach* himself. It is too difficult and impractical. Each freezer costs a lot of money, and how will the freezers be brought from place to place? These considerations did not deter Rav Aryeh. Because he was "removed from the fetters of the *self*," he could do things that other people cannot do. He simply carried the freezers himself from place to place.

Rav Aryeh personified the *middos* of Avraham and Rivka:

chessed without limits. Hashem took him from us because He wants us to know that this is what He desires in this world. *Chessed* without limits is the goal for which we are all meant to strive.

Preparing for Chanukah and Mashiach

CHAZAL TEACH US THAT THIRTY DAYS before a *chag* we should begin preparing ourselves by asking and hearing *drashos* about the halachos of the *chag*. The Har Nof Massacre took place on 25 Cheshvan, exactly one month before Chanukah.

The Bach (at the beginning of *hilchos Chanukah*) reveals that the *gezeirah* of Chanukah took place because of *hisrashlus b'avodah* — indolence in *avodas Hashem*. Hashem gave us thirty days before Chanukah to think about what happened and to strengthen our *avodah* — in all areas: Torah, *avodah* and *gemilus chassadim*.

Chevlei Mashiach

CHAZAL TELL US THAT IF WE WANT TO BE spared from *chevlei Mashiach*, the tribulations that precede Mashiach, we should involve ourselves in Torah and *gemilus chassadim*. We understand that to be *oseik b'Torah* means to learn Torah with all of one's strength and concentration, but what does *oseik bigemilus chassadim* mean? It means to do *chessed* without limits!

People might think: Either I can excel in Torah, or I can excel in *chessed*. There doesn't seem to be enough time in the day to do both. An account of Rav Shach's younger years shows the error in this reasoning:

An elderly man once came to the Ponevezh Yeshivah and said that he had studied in *cheder* with the Rosh Yeshivah,

Rav Shach. The *talmidim* asked this man to describe Rav Shach as a young *bachur,* and he told them, "Rav Shach was learning constantly, but everyone benefitted from his *chessed.*" Rav Shach taught us that it is altogether possible to be a *masmid atzum* and still do *chessed* without limits.

We, as the *talmidim* of Yeshivas Heichal HaTorah, are privileged to have a living example of *gadlus* in Torah and *gadlus* in *chessed.* Our Rosh Yeshivah, Rav Tzvi Kushelevsky, personifies greatness in both of these areas. May the Rosh Yeshivah have *arichus yamim veshanim* and *nachas* from all of his *talmidim.*

Let us take these days to look into our own lives. We are all children of Avraham Avinu, and we all have within us the ability to do *chessed* without limits as he did. Hashem has taken Aryeh from us because He wants us to learn from his actions that this is the way a Jew is meant to act.

The Greatest and the Smallest*

By Rabbi Daniel Yaakov Travis, shlita

RAV LEVINE HAD MANY, MANY *MAALOS*, BUT PERHAPS HIS greatest attribute was his humility. Rav Levine was fluent in the entire Torah, and for anything you would ask him — in *Shas*, halachah or *mussar* — the source was on his lips. He would mention the answer nonchalantly, as though it was no big deal that he knew everything. He exemplified *Chazal's* words, *"Lo pasak girsa mipumeih"* — Torah did not leave his mouth even for a moment.

Yet with all of this Torah knowledge, the word *"kavod"* was not even in his vocabulary. He was, as *Chazal* describe (*Shabbos* 105b), "the *gadol* of the *chaburah*," the greatest of all the *talmidim* in the *beis medrash,* and at the same time he was "the *katan* of the *chaburah*," the smallest of all the *talmidim* in the *beis medrash* therefore he carried himself with absolute simplicity and *pashtus.*

On the way to the *kevurah*, his nephew Rabbi Yehudah Kraft commented that the Chafetz Chaim states that if a person receives honor in this world it detracts from his reward in the Next World. During his lifetime Rav Levine truly fled from *kavod*. He goes to *Olam Haba* with all of his reward completely intact.

---

* This *hesped* was delivered on 27 Cheshvan 5775 at Kollel Toras Chaim.

Eved Hashem

RAV LEVINE WAS A COMPLETE AND DEVOTED *eved Hashem*. He cared deeply for his children and would make sure that they always got enough sleep. Yet his family related that he was always still up learning at 2 a.m., and that he would wake up every morning without exception for a *neitz* minyan.

Rav Levine was a *zariz*. Wherever he went it was with alacrity and enthusiasm, and with total devotion to serving Hashem. He went from mitzvah to mitzvah like an arrow being shot from a bow heading straight for the target. He lived and breathed the *Borei Olam*.

Rav Levine headed a weekly *Mesilas Yesharim chaburah* in the *kollel*. He lived the ideals of that *sefer*, and *mussar* was the essence of his life. Everything he did was just one straight path of righteousness.

Speaking to Hashem

RAV LEVINE DAVENED LIKE HE WAS STANDING directly in front of the *Shechinah*. He would raise his hands and engage in a conversation with the *Borei Olam*. I often davened next to him, and he would daven at length, often crying during the *tefillah*.

Each *brachah* of his *Shemoneh Esrei* was filled with passion and *kavanah*. During *tefillah* he appeared to be engaged in a war — a battle to raise his *emunah* higher and higher and to come to an absolute recognition of Hashem. He would turn to Hashem as a child cries to his parents, begging Him for help.

Chazal tell us that one should live every day as if it were his last. Rav Levine exemplified this, and whenever he davened it was as though this was his final *Shemoneh Esrei* in this world. The night before he was murdered, Rav Levine davened in the *kollel* with profound intensity, and watching him in prayer I was especially moved.

Guarding His Tongue RAV LEVINE GUARDED HIS TONGUE AS IF IT were a dangerous weapon. We once had a passionate, heated discussion about one of the halachos of *shemiras halashon*. In the end we agreed on the halachah, and during the course of this discussion I saw that not only did he know the halachos of *shemiras halashon*, he lived them.

Immediately after Rav Levine's *kevurah* one of his *talmidim* got up and gave a fiery *drashah*. He spoke about Rav Levine's exceptional *hasmadah* and *middos*. Even after a full day of crying, there were many more tears.

One of the most inspiring things he spoke about was Rav Levine's *shemiras halashon*. His *talmid* testified that you could not slip in a single word of *lashon hara* when talking to Rav Levine. He had a complete mastery of the halachos; they permeated his blood.

Emunah Sheleimah RAV RUBIN, THE RAV OF THE SHUL WHERE THE tragedy occurred, related that the way of the Jewish people is not to take revenge. The custom is to bury those who die *al kiddush Hashem* in their blood-stained clothes, and the Shach explains that the reason for this is that when the victim arrives in *Olam Haba* Hashem will see his blood-stained clothes. While we must defend ourselves, it is Hashem Who will take vengeance on our enemies.

Our job is to serve Hashem with complete *emunah*. The tests that we are experiencing now are all *nisyonos* in *emunah*.

Every individual has to think about what happened and how he can increase his *emunah* and return to Hashem in *teshuvah sheleimah*.

The Rav related that when he was learning in *kollel* they received a special visit from Rav Shach, who was by then very old and weak. Rav Shach leaned on the *bimah* and simply read the first *pesukim* of *Bereishis*, describing how Hashem created the entire world. Initially Rav Rubin was disappointed that this *gadol b'Torah* was relaying such a simple message, but in his later years the Rav understood the great depth of relating *emunah peshutah*, simple faith in Hashem.

Rav Levine lived with *emunah peshutah*, and it manifested itself in his every action. His *emunah* was complete, leaving not the slightest room for any doubt. Especially in the last year of his life, when there was so much clear *hashgachah pratis* being seen in Eretz Yisrael, Rav Levine spoke constantly about Hashem's miracles and how close Mashiach is.

Rabbi Levine's nephew Rabbi Yehudah Kraft told me about the great strength of his uncle's *almanah*. Rabbi Kraft had just made a *bris* a few days earlier, and his aunt had not yet seen him. Shortly after she heard of her husband's murder, Rebbetzin Levine still had the clarity of mind to wish her nephew *mazal tov* on the *bris*.

When her family heard that their father was gone, she forgot about her own pain and focused on comforting her children. "You lost your father," she said, "but you still have your mother." Seeing her great inner strength we can understand what the Levine family was about.

May Hashem comfort her, and all the families of the *kedoshim*, along with all the *almanos* and *yesomim* among our nation.

RAV KALMAN ZE'EV LEVINE *HY"D*

Eved Hashem

By Rebbetzin Chaya Levine

M Y HUSBAND'S GOAL IN LIFE WAS TO CONNECT TO Hashem through performing mitzvos and learning Torah to make the world a place full of Hashem's light and love.

My husband taught me that every person is created with tremendous potential to bring light and goodness to the world. Hashem created each person with unique *kochos* — talents, brains and personality traits. Focus on your talents and abilities.

Many of us give up on ourselves too soon because we focus on what is negative in ourselves and others. Many of us think we have to do big things to change ourselves and the world. It is our small acts that are going to make big differences.

My husband never gave up — he just kept going. One of his friends said something along the lines of, "We both sat in the same *beis medrash*. How did he get so far…?" He did it one step at a time, one *daf* at a time. If he wanted to change or improve something, he would pick one thing to work on, such as davening or *brachos*; he broke it up into specific steps and then chose one small thing to work on for months until he got it right. Then he would move on to the next step. He would supplement his efforts by learning about that *middah* or *brachah* from a *sefer*, as well as keeping a written record for himself. That way he could see how much he had improved and what to move on to next. We worked together on many such projects, halachically and *hashkafically*. When you get discouraged, just keep going — you'll get there in the end. He learned this from the teachings of Rav Wolbe, many of which were imparted to him by Rabbi Samsonovich, whose *mussar vaad* he still attended every Wednesday.

One of the great gifts G-d has given every one of us is the power of speech. Speech, by definition, is the ability to express thought and feeling, thereby giving physical form to a spiritual aspect of life. Like any *ko'ach*, it can be used to build the world or to destroy the world, to make positive connections or to cause separation.

For my husband, this expressed itself in his *avodah bein adam laMakom* in davening and in the way he communicated to others in his Torah learning. For him, davening was an opportunity to talk to G-d — our Father — Who loves us so much and is waiting to hear from us. If you need anything, who can better provide that than the all-powerful King Who can do anything? There was nothing too small or big to daven for; and anytime anything went right — "*Hodu laHashem ki tov!*" was his response.

If he had to do something difficult, or if there was an important decision to make, he always davened first — either with a request of his own or by saying *Tehillim*. If we had a *tzarah*, he davened. If we had a *simchah*, he davened. If an ambulance went by, if someone told him of their *tzarah*, whether or not he could do anything about it, he davened for them. I had to daven for forty days in a row at the Kosel to be *zocheh* to marry him.

He was also particular about saying *brachos* with *kavanah*. He would stop what he was doing and hold the food in his right hand and say the *brachah* aloud, careful to pronounce and concentrate on G-d's Name and on "*Melech ha'olam.*" He was truly grateful to Hashem for all that He gave us. He said *Asher yatzar* from a siddur. That was his *hishtadlus* for good health. All of *tefillah* was active *hishtadlus* to him.

When it came to *bein adam lachaveiro*, he used speech to connect to people and to build people up; he never used it for cutting people down or hurting them. He was against using nicknames and never told a joke at the expense of another person or group. He only spoke well of others and refused to speak negatively about anyone. Because he was so committed to speaking only well of others, it trained him to think only well of others, so that over time it became natural for him. He did this because he knew that every person is created *betzelem Elokim*, which means that everyone has an innate desire to be good and to do good — it's just that sometimes we mess up. He believed in that goodness and never gave up on his *talmidim*, his children or anyone else.

He reviewed the halachos often and encouraged us to do the same. He never repeated "news items" unless it was a *simchah*. He greeted people with a smile. He was also accurate in his speech and did not lie. He never revealed things told to him in private. He just never spoke about people.

The third way he used his speech was in Torah learning. That was a way to connect to G-d and to his *talmidim*. It was also the way to create clarity and build the world, to bring Hashem closer to this world. Anyone who came to Kehilat Bnei Torah on Simchas Torah remembers the way he danced and the joy on his face — he was so grateful to Hashem for the opportunity he had to learn Torah, to serve Hashem, for the beauty of the world, for all Hashem did for us. This was the source of his *simchah*. It is no coincidence that Rosh Chodesh Kislev was during the *shivah* and that the *shloshim* came out on 25/26 Kislev.

His Torah and *avodas Hashem* filled the world with light and brought joy to anyone who knew him.

No one can extinguish his light or the light of any of the other kedoshim — the light of the Jewish people or the light of Mashiach. Let us bring that light closer by taking upon ourselves one action to emulate my husband. Let us increase the light by accepting upon ourselves to use our speech properly.

Please choose one practical step that you can take to bring light to our world.

A Life of Extraordinary *Avodas Hashem**

By Rav Levine's son-in-law,
Rabbi Eli Pelkovitz, shlita

I WOULD LIKE TO SPEAK A BIT ABOUT THE *YAMIM NORA'IM* with my father-in-law, Rav Kalman. On Yom Kippur we used to daven *neitz* together. One Yom Kippur I accidently set my alarm to go off an hour early; instead of ringing at 4 a.m., it rang at 3 a.m. I decided to go to shul then, so that I wouldn't fall back to sleep and risk missing the *neitz* minyan. I arrived an hour before davening was to begin, and I was the second person there. Rav Kalman greeted me.

His davening during the *Yamim Nora'im* was extraordinary. On Rosh Hashanah and Yom Kippur his *Shemoneh Esrei* would last between 80 and 100 minutes. Rav Elephant, a *maggid shiur* in Mir-Yerushalayim and a resident of Har Nof, said that on Yom Kippur Rav Kalman davened like a *nefesh b'li guf* — a soul without a body. When he recited *vidui* he had multiple siddurim open before him, to ensure that he would say *vidui* with maximum *kavanah*.

This past Motzaei Yom Kippur I was *zocheh* to learn with Rav Kalman in a *kollel* from 9:30 to 11 p.m. Despite the day's

---

* This *hesped* was delivered on 10 Kislev 5775 in Beis Kenesses Ahavas Torah.

exhausting *avodah*, he was able to ask very strong questions on the *Rosh* in *Shevi'is*. One Sukkos he came down with a bad cold. He told me that it was probably because he hadn't been able to fall asleep after Yom Kippur, since he was still flying from the *avodas hayom*.

This past year he told me that during *Selichos* he decided to say only one of the *piyutim*, joining the *tzibbur* during their recitation of the Thirteen *Middos*, to fulfill the halachah set forth in the *Shulchan Aruch* that it is better to pray a little with *kavanah* than to pray a lot without *kavanah*.

His *ayin tovah* — his ability to see the good in all people — was amazing. He had something good to say about everyone. I would joke that, judging by his words, I couldn't tell who in the yeshivah was a *bachur* and who was a *maggid shiur*, who were the *avreichim* and who were the *ramim*, since he praised everyone so effusively. To give a typical example, on Pesach last year the refrigerator was broken. The next time I saw him he had a whole laundry list of nice things to say about the repairman — he was on time, he was a real *ben Torah*, he did the work for a good price, etc., etc.

His *emunas chachamim* was in a class by itself. Everyone in the family knew that he was very careful about doing whatever the *rabbanim* said. After he was *niftar*, some of the family members wanted a separate funeral; others disagreed. The discussion ended when one son said that Abba would have done whatever Rav Rubin said.

When my first son was born, I asked Rav Chaim Kanievsky, *shlita*, what he should be named. When I told Rav Kalman that Rav Chaim had chosen the name, he was so overjoyed that for the next two weeks he ran around telling everyone that the *Urim V'tumim* had named his grandchild.

Another particularly special memory I have is that during the *seudah* every Purim, about ten minutes before *shekiah*, the family would say *Tehillim*. This time is considered to be an *eis ratzon*, an auspicious time for prayer, and afterwards Rav Kalman would say a *Mi shebeirach* for people who were ill and for girls who needed *shidduchim*.

His life was a kaleidoscope of *avodas Hashem* and *ahavas Yisrael*. May his memory be a true inspiration to every one of us.

RAV KALMAN ZE'EV LEVINE *HY"D*

And It Will Be for a Sign...

By Rabbi Moshe Michael Tzoren, shlita

W E SPOKE TO THE CHILDREN OF RABBI KALMAN LEVINE, *Hy"d*, who was the first martyred victim of the Har Nof terror attack. His second oldest son, whose wedding was five months ago, told us an amazing story.

"At Shamgar (funeral home), after I identified Abba, before the funeral procession set out, several people who had taken care of Abba told me they had a surprise for me. I didn't know what they meant, but suddenly they presented me with a bag, and in it were the tefillin of my father, *Hy"d*.

"'The tefillin of the other victims had to be buried with them,' they told me, 'due to the blood on them, but your father's tefillin *battim* were left intact and clean, without even a drop of blood.'"

The straps did need burial, but the *battim* remained untainted.

In a conversation, the Levine family mentioned that their father had said a number of times that he never spoke about everyday matters while wearing tefillin. "He almost never engaged in mundane conversation in any case," his children related, "but with tefillin — we too can testify that we never once saw him do such a thing."

A Tribute to a *Gadol**

By Rav Moshe Meiselman, shlita
Rosh Yeshivah of Yeshivas Toras Moshe

THE WORLD IS REELING FROM THE TRAGIC SLAUGHTER OF the four *kedoshei elyon* who were brutally murdered while they were standing before *Hakadosh Baruch Hu* in *tefillah*. Someone who is killed because he is a Jew is a *kadosh* who dies *al kiddush Hashem*. The Gemara tells us that he deserves the title of *kadosh* even more if he lived his life *al kiddush Hashem*.

Among the *kedoshei elyon*, Rabbi Moshe Twersky was a *gadol baTorah* and a *tzaddik* in every way. For the past twenty-two years he was *marbitz Torah* in Yeshivas Toras Moshe in Yerushalayim. He raised countless *talmidim* to very great heights in Torah and *yiras Shamayim*. Today his *talmidim* are all over the world. They looked up to him, for they saw in him the true embodiment of all the ideals of the Torah.

He was a descendant of two great dynasties — the dynasty of Chernobyl-Tolner and the dynasty of Brisk. The intellectual brilliance and command of Torah that signified Brisk was natural and automatic to him. He toiled in Torah

---

* This *hesped* was delivered on 25 Cheshvan 5775 at the *levayah* of Rav Moshe Twersky.

until late in the night. He knew major portions of *Shas* by heart, and the rest was at his fingertips. Every one of his *talmidim* felt his love, and he treated them as his own sons. His sons were his *talmidim* and his *talmidim* were his sons.

He was a unique person in that he was just as scrupulous about *chumros* in *mitzvos bein adam lechaveiro* as he was in *mitzvos bein adam laMakom*. The *avodah* of Chassidus burned deeply in him, and he sought out *gedolei ha'avodah* to inspire him and to learn from them the nuances of *avodah*. This is what brought him to master *Kabbalah* as well, and that is unique to someone so steeped in the traditions of Brisk.

The *hespedim* emphasized time and again the true purity of soul that dominated his life. He was a *talmid* of his grandfather, Rav Yosef Dov Soloveitchik, *zt"l*, and of Rav Dovid Soloveitchik, *shlita*, and in *Kabbalah*, of Rav Yisrael Eliyahu Weintraub, *zt"l*. They all saw in him their true *talmid*, for whom they had a deep respect filled with awe.

Klal Yisrael has suffered a great loss with the departure of a future *Gadol* whose *shleimus* in Torah, *avodah* and *gemilus chassadim* was recognized by everyone who came within his presence. *Gedolim* are few and far between, and when a future *Gadol* departs from us before he has reached his prime, it is an irretrievable loss. *Mi yitein lanu temuraso!*

RAV MOSHE TWERSKY *HY"D*

Thoughts and Recollections of a *Talmid**

By Rabbi Eliezer Menachem Niehaus, shlita

As I poured bag after bag of dirt into the grave of my *rebbeh, Hakadosh Hagaon* Harav Moshe Twersky, *zt"l, Hashem yinkom damo,* I felt as if I was burying a part of myself as well. I wished I could just pinch myself and wake up from this nightmare. The memories of those first years, when I was a 17-year-old *bachur* in Yeshivas Toras Moshe, were all coming back. Even back then everyone knew he was a huge *talmid chacham,* a *masmid,* an extreme *medakdek* in mitzvos, a major *lamdan,* a tzaddik and a *heilege Yid!* We revered him and viewed him as a *malach,* but at the same time we loved him dearly; I know this sounds like a contradiction — but that was truly the case! When I received the call with the horrible news, the phone dropped from my hand and I cried as I had never cried before. During the *shivah,* a fellow *talmid* from those days called me from England, and we cried together. We both expressed the same feeling: Part of us is now gone. What was it about the *rebbeh,* as we referred to him fondly, that made him so beloved to all his *talmidim?*

---

* A version of this article first appeared in the *Kuntris Magazine,* Kislev 5775.

Each *talmid* might give a different explanation, but I am sure that there are some points on which everyone would agree. The first thing that comes to mind — and I miss it so dearly — is that huge, warm smile that he gave everyone he met, and especially his *talmidim*. It was so obvious that it flowed from the true *ahavas Yisrael* that his great heart felt for every Yid. But we as his *talmidim* felt his genuine concern for us, so much so that each of us felt like his only son. Whenever we met he would always ask me how my family was doing. Once I asked him to daven for a family member who was not well, and the next time we spoke, which was quite some time later, his first question was about that family member!

But his concern for us did not end with that smile; he always knew what to say to make us feel good about ourselves. When we needed encouragement, he was the one we turned to. At one point I was learning in a *kollel* whose *Rosh Kollel* was an absolute genius. Every *pshat* I suggested in the *sugya*, he would destroy with several pointed questions and would then give his own "*iluyish*" *pshat* that did not sit well with me. I was getting quite depressed, because I was left without any *pshat* in the *sugya* at all! So I called the *rebbeh*, and he told me not to worry. Hear his questions and try to answer them, *rebbeh* said, but you don't have to accept his *pshat*.

Last Chanukah I went to America for a family *simchah*. Since this was the first time I was leaving Eretz Yisrael in almost eight years, I left a few days early in order to do some fund-raising for our night *kollel*. It was hard for me to leave my family and Eretz Yisrael, so as I was waiting at the airport I called the *rebbeh* for *chizuk* and a *brachah*. I can still hear his words ringing in my ears: "It's a good sign if you're traveling with a heavy heart — you will definitely be *matzliach*!" And, *baruch Hashem*, I was!

The *rebbeh* was the one who encouraged me to open the night *kollel* in Kiryat Sefer, almost fifteen years ago, and he told us exactly how we should be learning. Whenever questions arose we would discuss them with him, and his name appeared on the *kollel* stationery as the Rabbinical advisor. Any time I called him he would ask me about the *kollel* and where we were up to in our learning. It was clearly in his heart. When we made our first *siyum*, he came out to Kiryat Sefer and gave a *drashah*. To this day, we remember how he kept repeating that he was jealous of us, and what a big *chizuk* it was for him to come! Small, simple words, but their impact lasted forever, because they were said with true, sincere feeling.

On the last day of the *shivah*, the *kollel* members asked me to say a *hesped* in the *kollel*. I began with the *gemara* in *Shabbos* (153a) that relates that Rav told Rav Shmuel bar Shilas, "Achim b'hespeidah d'hasam ka'imna." Rashi explains that this means that he told him, "Invest great effort into how you say the *hesped* for me after I die so that you will arouse the emotions of the listeners and cause them to cry, *because I will be there listening.*" When I said those words, the thought that the *rebbeh's heiligeh neshamah* was with us in the room caused me to be so overcome with emotion that I simply could not continue speaking. But then I pictured him smiling and saying, "Don't worry, I'm sure you'll do a good job," and that gave me the strength to continue saying the *hesped*. That is how he was when he was alive, and that is what stayed in my heart.

Another reason we so cherished him was that there was

so much in him to admire and look up to. We viewed him as a living *Shulchan Aruch*. Everything he did was with a *cheshbon* and according to halachah. We would work on figuring out why he did certain things and what was the *makor* for them. Then we would try to get him to tell us if that was the case. We were not always successful, as he never liked to talk about himself. But although he was so great, he was at the same time so normal — a human being like all of us — and therefore we hoped and strived to be like him.

And finally, he gave us the ability to work on reaching our full potential in Torah and *avodas Hashem*. After *shiur* I would go to him and ask him why he had explained something a certain way and not the way I had understood it. With great patience he would show me where I had gone wrong and why his way was the proper way to understand the *sugya*.

He would drop a little comment here and there if he felt we could be doing more or learning more, but always in a positive way. On one occasion he told me, "Eliezer, it's time for you to start filling notebooks of your own *chiddushim*! Don't just write over the *shiurim* you hear, write a summary of the *sugya* with your understanding of the *Rishonim*." That small piece of advice planted a seed inside of me that is still growing to this very day!

Once he came in to *shiur* on *erev Shavuos* with a glow on his face. "Last night," he said, "we counted the forty-ninth day of *sefiras ha'omer*. We should have been so full of joy after finishing a mitzvah that took forty-nine days to complete that we should have started to dance!" That small exclamation made such an impact on me that today, almost twenty years later, before I count the last night of *sefirah* I recall what he said, and it makes such a difference in the way I count!

That was his incredible *ko'ach* as a rebbi; he had the ability to instill in his *talmidim* little ideas that would continue to grow and grow. The reason these ideas were so deeply embedded in our hearts was that we recognized that every word he said came from his remarkable *middas ha'emes* and his burning desire for perfection in everything he did — the learning of Torah, meticulousness in mitzvos, and *avodas hatefillah*.

To convey a full picture of his vast greatness is nearly impossible, because most of it was hidden from our eyes, and what we did see was truly indescribable. In his passing, the loss was not only for us, his *talmidim*, but for all of *Klal Yisrael*. It is possible to say that Hashem took him in such a horrifying way not only to arouse everyone to do *teshuvah*, but also to reveal his greatness to the entire world. Now everyone saw that it is possible in our times to reach levels of greatness that are reminiscent of previous generations.

I might have ended with the words, "The *rebbeh* is not here anymore — who can replace him?" but I can hear him exclaiming, "What do you mean? Each and every one of you can be just like me, if not greater!"

A *Talmid's* View

By Rabbi Yehoshua Berman, shlita

T HE *MESILAS YESHARIM* TEACHES THAT THE HIGHEST levels of *avodas Hashem* are not generally reached by most Jews. However, in the *zechus* of those *yechidei segulah* who do in fact achieve those pinnacles of devotion and dedication, the entire *Klal Yisrael* is uplifted. Those rare individuals who accomplish so much in their *avodas Hashem* are in fact *Klal Yisrael* at its best.

Rav Moshe Twersky was one of those *yechidei segulah*.

Astounding Hasmadah PERHAPS HIS GREATEST FACET WAS HIS UN-fathomable devotion to learning Torah. *Chazal* tell us that there is someone called a *Sinai* — the phenomenal *baki* who is so fluent in every detail of *kol haTorah kulah*; and there is an *Oker Harim*, the *lamdan* whose astonishing brilliance and clarity simply dazzles the mind. It is so rare to meet someone who embodies both of these characteristics, but Rav Moshe Twersky did just that. You could not catch him off-guard in anything related to Torah learning. No matter what passage in *Shas* — or any other area of Torah learning — you would start discussing with him, it would seem as though he had just now finished learning that *sugya*. Even in the subtle details — the *diyuk* in

Rashi, the *machlokes* about how to understand *shitas haRambam*, or the three approaches of the *Acharonim* on the *sugya*, including the *makom iyun* on each one — he was intimately familiar with it. Torah was his life, in the most literal sense.

Rebbi never went to lunch. He would have a little snack, but he didn't eat lunch. He loved learning so much that he simply could not be bothered to leave it to go have a meal in the middle of the day. I once heard from an *adam gadol* that there are very few people whom "you could just put in the middle of a *midbar* with a Gemara and a *shtender* and they'd be happy. Rav Moshe Twersky is one of them."

Rebbi's *hasmadah* was phenomenal. He once told me, "It *is* possible to learn more when you're married. For most people it's the opposite, but it is possible." This statement also speaks volumes about, *tibadeil l'chaim*, his Rebbetzin, who was clearly a major part of the secret behind Rebbi's phenomenal accomplishments.

"In my entire life," Rebbi's son Meshulam said at the *levayah*, "I never once saw my father go to sleep on Shabbos. On occasion I would wake up in the middle of the night, around 2 a.m., and I would see him learning." Rebbi's son Avraham added, "My father told me that the time on Shabbos is just too precious, and therefore he simply could not use it for sleep."

A Gaon in Human Relations

REBBI WAS INCREDIBLY DEVOTED TO HIS *talmidim*. He learned privately with so many *talmidim* over the years, in addition to the innumerable *shiurim* that he delivered and the night *sedarim* that he spent answering questions. One time during *shiur*, after explaining a certain point, he said, "Are there any questions? Now's the time to ask!" He wasn't just teaching Gemara. He was teaching *talmidim*. His concern was that they should understand. If they didn't, he would take the time to explain it again… and again, if necessary, even if that meant that he wouldn't get to the next topic that he wanted to delve into that day.

There were *talmidim* who at times would ask him any random question that occurred to them. Rebbi never brushed off a question. If it was a question on his personal *hanhagos*, which he wanted very much to keep private, he might sidestep it. But to brush off any other question as being silly or irrelevant — never. His respect and concern for his *talmidim* was just too great for that.

Once, he saw a *talmid* sitting outside to soak up some sun during *bein hasedarim*. Rebbi immediately warned the *bachur* that sitting too long in the sun could be dangerous. The *bachur*, who was independent and strong-minded, didn't take the warning seriously. Rebbi reiterated his point gently and left it at that. His concern for his *talmidim* was all-encompassing, but he would not force his opinion on others even if it was so obviously correct.

Amazingly, this is how Rebbi acted when it came to teaching Torah as well. After suggesting several solutions to a question, he would often say, *"V'habocher yivchar,"* encouraging his *talmidim* to choose whichever solution they preferred. He spoke this way to 19-year-old *bachurim* who could not begin to approach his breadth of knowledge and depth of understanding. If a *talmid* argued with his *pshat*, he would not forcefully show the *talmid* where he had erred. Rather, he would cultivate in his *talmidim* independence of thought, enabling them to develop their own abilities. He was an absolute giant in Torah scholarship, but what a gentle giant he was!

On one occasion, Rebbi was speaking to me about how certain days are auspicious for davening, such as Rosh Chodesh, Chanukah and Purim. I confided that this pressure often made me nervous, and as a result I'd have less *kavanah* on a day like that. "In that case," said Rebbi, "you should just think of it as any regular day!" Every special calendar day was incredibly precious to Rebbi; *avodah* was real and alive for him, and he worked hard to maximize these special times. Nonetheless, he related to others on their level, even if that meant telling them to "treat it like any regular day!"

At one point a certain man who was "not all there" frequented Rebbi's house. Odd behavior was the norm for this unfortunate individual. Not only was Rebbi friendly and patient with this person, he treated him with respect, showing him that he was valued and held in esteem. Even if the man said something inappropriate, Rebbi would simply incline his head to acknowledge that something was said, without indicating agreement to the statement; but he would not correct him. *Kavod* for others was just too important to Rebbi.

One year on Purim, he spoke extensively about *hakaras hatov*. He applied it, on a practical level, to appreciating the Rebbetzin. It was she, after all, who had prepared the entire *seudah*. The following *leil Shabbos* he hosted many *bachurim*, as he usually did, and the meal ended late. We thanked him and left. On our way out of the building, I mentioned to the *bachur* who was walking with me, "We forgot to thank the Rebbetzin." He agreed that we should return to the house to thank her.

We knocked on the door, and when Rebbi opened it,

he had a quizzical look on his face. "We forgot to thank the Rebbetzin," we explained, and his eyes lit up with joy. Rather than simply telling us that he'd relay the message, then saying good Shabbos and leaving it at that, he invited us back in, offered us a seat, and prepared a bowl of ice cream for each of us (although we had already had ice cream for dessert at the end of the *seudah*).

Although we protested, he felt he absolutely had to reward what he considered to be such a wonderful effort on our part. We were really quite full — the Rebbetzin is a wonderful cook — and were not at all interested in more ice cream. Furthermore, we didn't feel that our returning to thank his wife was such a big deal; but Rebbi insisted. He felt he had to give us that positive reinforcement. When he finally set the two bowls down, though, he said, "If you really don't want it, you don't have to eat it." But how could we refuse?!

A Perfect Synthesis

REBBI WAS A DESCENDANT OF CHERNOBYL AND Tolner on his father's side. He had learned *Toras haChassidus*, and it was a strong part of him. On his mother's side, he was a grandson and close *talmid* of Rav Yosef Dov Soloveitchik (of Boston). He had also learned under Rav Dovid Soloveitchik (of Yerushalayim). The Torah of the Beis Halevi, Rav Chaim and the Brisker Rav was in his blood; he lived and breathed their Torah and their *mesorah*. Yet we never saw any contradictions between these approaches. In his singularly unique way, he synthesized the analytical prowess of Brisk with the fire of Chernobyl and Tolner, even in *machshavah*, *hashkafah* and *hanhagah*. He made everything fit together seamlessly. He was a paradigm of *Torah lishmah* and *talmud Torah k'neged kulam* combined with complete *hislahavus* and *mesirus nefesh* in *avodas Hashem*.

And all this was without fanfare. As Rav Moshe Meiselman, Rosh Yeshivah of Yeshivas Toras Moshe and Rebbi's close relative, expressed so succinctly, "He never made a fuss about himself. Many people have different 'audiences' in their life. Rav Moshe Twersky, though, had but one audience: the *Ribbono shel Olam*."

Rebbi's son Avraham mentioned that his father had invested tremendous effort in his *avodas Hashem*, taking on many *hiddurim* and *chumros*, but he had warned Avraham emphatically never to tell anyone about them. "Once, following one of these spectacular efforts," Avraham related, "my father said to me, 'Do you think that we are any better than anyone else because of what we just did? Not at all! We did what we did because that is what we understood to be necessary and the right thing to do. But it doesn't make us one iota better than anyone else!'" Rebbi acted with extraordinary *mesirus nefesh* for Torah and *dikduk b'mitzvos* at the highest level, while at the same time insisting, "I am no better than anyone else."

At a *sheva brachos*, Rebbi explained that on the words "*Lo baShamayim hi* — It is not in the Heavens" (*Devarim* 30:12), Rashi explains, "If the Torah were in *Shamayim*, we would have to go there to get it." Rebbi praised the *chassan* as being that type of person: If Torah would be in *Shamayim*, he would actually go there to get it. It seemed to me that Rebbi was describing a characteristic that resonated powerfully within himself, for in truth, that is exactly the way Rebbi related to Torah and *avodas Hashem*. He pushed himself far, far beyond normal human limits. Torah was his lifeblood. He absolutely had to have it, and he would do whatever was necessary to get it — he would even go to *Shamayim* if he had to.

Now Rebbi is in *Shamayim*, occupying his incredible place in the *Yeshivah shel Maalah*, while we are left behind, reeling from the trauma of the horrific tragedy and our indescribable loss. Perhaps we can gain a measure of comfort from something Rebbi himself once said in the wake of another horrific tragedy. After 9/11, at that time of intense sorrow, we were all looking for solace and direction. "Rebbi," I asked him, "what are we supposed to do?" Rebbi's response was simple and short, but contained a depth of meaning that touches the deepest places of the *neshamah*. "Talk to Hashem. I don't mean during *Shemoneh Esrei*; I mean to just talk to Him."

Intellectually, we realize that we are like the person looking through the keyhole in a hospital, and all he sees is a hand holding a knife and cutting into someone's body. We cannot see more than that, so to us it looks like outright murder. Of course, we know that Hashem knows what He is doing and that everything is ultimately for our good, but that awareness is way up in the abstract realm of our rational thinking. Our emotions, though, are heaving and throbbing with pain, and that intense anguish is our reality down here in the *olam ha'maaseh*. So what are we to do?

Talk to Hashem

WE NEED TO BE ABLE TO FEEL THAT, DESPITE all the incomprehensible pain and destruction, even in the depths of tragedy, Hashem is with us, that He never leaves go of us. This is perhaps one of the greatest lessons I ever learned from Rebbi: *Talk to Hashem.* Share your pain with Him. As hard as it is, allow yourself to connect with Him even in your most difficult moments, for that is where you will find strength and solace.

Rebbi was a legend in his lifetime to those relative few who were privileged to know him. Now, with his passing, his memory will become a tremendous *kiddush Hashem* — just as he lived his whole life. Now all of *Klal Yisrael* will know of this incredible, beautiful facet of its existence that was manifest in his amazing personality.

Rebbi, your presence in this world is and will forever be sorely missed, until Mashiach arrives. We yearn for that day to come very soon.

From one of your *talmidim*, forever.

MESSAGES

"Each of us must strengthen himself as much as possible in Torah and chessed, following the guidance of Hillel, who taught, 'What you do not like, do not do to your friend.'"

– Rosh Hayeshivah Rav Aharon Leib Steinman, shlita

A Message from the Rosh Hayeshivah
Rav Aharon Leib Steinman, *shlita*

WE CANNOT POSSIBLY UNDERSTAND THE WISDOM OF Heaven; there is no way to answer the question of why Hashem would treat us in such a harsh manner. Yet we must accept the fact that Hashem does absolutely everything with very precise calculations, tempering His every act with mercy.

Chazal tell us, "What should a person do to save himself from the *chevlei Mashiach*?" Rashi explains that the coming of Mashiach will be accompanied by tremendous suffering, like a woman giving birth. *Chazal* answer that one should involve oneself in Torah and *gemilus chassadim*. Therefore, each of us must strengthen himself as much as possible in Torah and *chessed*, following the guidance of Hillel, who taught, "What you do not like, do not do to your friend."

Let everyone return to Hashem through *teshuvah*, and each individual knows in which area he needs to strengthen himself. Then Hashem's anger will subside, and we will no longer hear of such vicious attacks.

> With great empathy for all those of *Klal Yisrael* who have suffered personally from this attack,
>
> Rav Aharon Leib Steinman
> 26 Cheshvan 5775

In Response to "The Destruction of the World"

By the Rosh Hayeshivah
Rav Aharon Steinman, shlita, at the end of the shivah

IN *MELACHIM II* (21:16) IT IS RELATED, "MENASHE ALSO SHED much innocent blood, until he filled Yerushalayim with it from end to end, aside from his sin of causing Yehudah to sin, to do what was evil in Hashem's Eyes."

In *maseches Sanhedrin* (103a) *Chazal* explain that this refers to Menashe's murder of Yeshayahu Hanavi. Rashi comments, "…this is according to the opinion that he killed Yeshayahu — and the description of filling Yerushalayim from end to end with blood is justified, because the sin of murdering a tzaddik is equal to having filled all of Yerushalayim with the dead!"

We see here that *if one tzaddik is taken away, that is equivalent to the destruction of the world*! In our days, to our sorrow, we have seen this happen in the context of our generation. We cannot be likened to the generation of Yeshahayu Hanavi, but relative to our generation, the loss of these tzaddikim is like the destruction of the world.

People were killed in their tallis and tefillin, while davening; an enormous tragedy has befallen us in our generation.

Each of us must learn from this and make substantial improvements in his commitment to Torah and *yiras Shamayim*. If we will do this, I am certain that *Hakadosh Baruch Hu* will protect us so that we will experience no more sorrow.

Why Did This Tragedy Happen?*

By Rav Moshe Sternbuch, shlita
Rosh Av Beis Din Yerushalayim

THOSE OF US WHO LIVE IN HAR NOF ARE DEVASTATED. WE can still hear the piercing screams of the children who, for many hours, did not know whether their parents were alive or dead, crying, "Abba, Abba, we want you back!" Hours later they learned the truth; Hashem had carried out the harshest of decrees on their fathers.

It is impossible for us to understand the ways of Hashem, Who took these four tzaddikim from among us. We stood with them daily, side by side, and witnessed their unwavering devotion to Torah, *tefillah*, *chessed* and every other area of *avodas Hashem*. How can we possibly fathom why Hashem chose them to be taken from us?

However, it is not for us to judge Hashem's ways, as the *navi* tells us: His thoughts are not like ours, and His ways are not like ours, for as high as the Heavens are above the land, so too are Hashem's ways and His thoughts so far beyond our comprehension (see *Yeshayahu* 55:8-9). Hashem is a just and righteous G-d, and we have the ability to rectify the transgressions that may have led to this horrific incident.

---

* This *hesped* is an excerpt from a *drashah* that Rav Sternbuch delivered on 27 Cheshvan 5775, two days after the massacre. All four of the *kedoshim* were regular *mispallelim* at the shul of the Rav.

If we will analyze the events, it will become clear that it all happened as a result of our actions, and that it was strict Divine justice punishing us for our sins. This is the way of Hashem's *middas hadin*; it does not let transgressions go unpunished. When the Jewish people sin, the *middas hadin* seeks retribution against all of the Jewish people, but Hashem in His infinite mercy is not willing to unleash the full force of His wrath upon us. Instead, He appeases it with the death of tzaddikim, who act as a choice offering in our place.

Asarah Harugei Malchus — ten righteous tzaddikim, including Rabi Akiva, were brutally murdered. At that time Hashem took the holiest of the nation, the *kedoshim* and *gedolim* of that time. We too have experienced Hashem's punishment for our sins, for He has taken tzaddikim from among us as *korbanos*. Each of these four *kedoshim* who were killed is a *korban olah*, and it is their blood that has stopped the *middas hadin* from taking vengeance on all of *Klal Yisrael*.

Hashem Is Calling Out to Us

IN ORDER TO PUT THIS IN PERSPECTIVE, WE must analyze the backdrop of what took place. "All the nations of the world will see that the Name of Hashem is upon you, and they will fear you" (*Devarim* 28:10). *Chazal* reveal to us that this refers to the tefillin that are worn on the head.

At the time of the attack, all the members of the shul were wearing tallis and tefillin. They were standing before the *Shechinah*, in the midst of davening *Shemoneh Esrei*. They were in a shul, which is a *mikdash me'at*, a small Beis Hamikdash, where Hashem's Presence rests. In this powerful venue of *kedushah* and Divine protection, how is it possible that such a tragedy could occur?

We no longer have prophecy, and there is no way to discern exactly what Hashem wants from us. However, we know that "Nothing happens in this world unless there is first a heavenly decree" (*Chullin* 7b). Hashem has shaken up the Jewish people — and the purpose of such tragedies is to wake us up and to inspire us to make an intensive *cheshbon hanefesh*. If we do not take action now and change our ways, other calamities could follow, *Rachmana litzlan*.

"If you relate to Me with indifference (*b'keri*) and do not obey Me, I will afflict you with seven times what you deserve for your transgressions" (*Vayikra* 26:21). If we attribute what happened to chance and do not take it as an impetus to bring us to *teshuvah*, then Hashem's anger will increase exponentially, and we will need even more losses to appease the *middas hadin*. Every Jew must take these events to heart and must return to Hashem, and we will then see that "He is Merciful; He forgives sins and will not destroy. He holds back His rage exceedingly and does not release all His anger" (*Tehillim* 78:38).

During World War I, when the Cossacks in the Ukraine murdered tens of thousands of Jews, the Chafetz Chaim called upon all the *rabbanim* of Europe to declare a day of fasting for all of the Jewish people. All of the *rabbanim* signed on this request, with the exception of Rav Chaim Brisker. Rav Chaim explained that there is no point in making such a fast unless it is prefaced by *teshuvah*. Therefore, the first thing that needed to be done was to have all of the *rabbanim* gather and decide in which areas *Klal Yisrael* needed strengthening and what the Jewish people were capable of doing.

"Let us examine our ways, and return to Hashem" (*Eichah* 3:40). We too must follow Rav Chaim's directive and investigate which aspects of *avodas Hashem* are in need of repair. We cannot understand what Hashem is asking of us; we can only mention a few areas that are in need of strengthening.

Before doing so we must make two fundamental points. The first is that, although Torah learning is the mainstay of *Klal Yisrael*, after having experienced such a tragedy and offered such *korbanos*, it is not sufficient merely to strengthen ourselves in Torah learning. Rather, we must make a thorough *cheshbon hanefesh* and try to understand where our weaknesses lie, and what we can do to repair them.

Secondly, we must remember what Rav Nissim Gaon wrote in his introduction to his *Vidui*, said on Yom Kippur Katan: "*Ribbono shel Olam*, there is not enough time in my life to admit and ask forgiveness for all the transgressions that I have committed...." Even if we focus on specific sins, it would be impossible for us to know exactly why Hashem has brought this upon us.

Pursuing Peace

ONE AREA THAT SORELY NEEDS OUR ATTENTION is distancing ourselves from *machlokes*. The situation in Eretz Yisrael has deteriorated to the point that some people refuse to marry other Jews, will not count other Jews as part of a minyan, will not rely on other Jews to be witnesses for *kiddushin*, and separate themselves from other Jews in all areas of Jewish life. Even great *talmidei chachamim* have been sucked into this pattern of *machlokes*, and the situation continues to become more and more dire.

While our people have had many internal disputes throughout Jewish history, the current fierce political *machlokes* has become particularly embittered. As we speak, it is dividing our great yeshivos, causing conflict within families and across generations, and undermining the common goals of the Torah community.

Some people dismiss it as "just politics," but the pain brought about by one group of Jews condemning another is never merely a political issue. It is a spiritual issue that concerns us all deeply.

Before trying to understand how we can rectify this tragic situation, we must clarify an important issue: The Gemara is filled with disputes. *Chazal* tell us that the *machlokes* between Beis Shamai and Beis Hillel is the prototype of a *machlokes l'sheim Shamayim* (*Avos* 5:17). How can we tell whether a *machlokes* is *l'sheim Shamayim* and should be encouraged, or is not *l'sheim Shamayim* and must be ended?

Chazal tell us that the quintessential *machlokes* that is not *l'sheim Shamayim* is the *machlokes* of Korach and his *eidah*. At first glance it is difficult to understand why Korach's *machlokes* was not *l'sheim Shamayim*. Korach was 100 percent convinced that he was correct and that Moshe Rabbeinu was wrong. For this reason, Korach was willing to put his life on the line and undergo the test of whose incense would be accepted. Korach must have been sure that he would be chosen to be the *kohen gadol*; otherwise he would not have been willing to submit himself to a test that put his life at risk.

There are other proofs that Korach was an extremely holy and sincere person. Although Korach and his followers were swallowed up, their *machtos* were preserved and made into a cover for the *Mizbei'ach*. The *Midrash Tanchuma* (*Korach* 12) adds that Korach had *ruach hakodesh*.

The Arizal teaches that Korach will be the *kohen gadol* in the Third Beis Hamikdash. His greatness is hinted to in the last letters of the words "*Tzaddik katamar yifrach*" (*Tehillim*

92:13), which spell out the name Korach. This indicates that Korach's greatness will become apparent in the end of days. We must ask, therefore, after all of these proofs of his righteousness, how can *Chazal* label Korach's dispute with Moshe Rabbeinu the ultimate *machlokes* that is not *l'sheim Shamayim*?

It is well-known that Hashem loathes *machlokes*. As such, anyone who engages in a dispute with another religious Jew is doing so with the understanding that even if he is correct he is causing great anguish to the *Borei Olam*. It is incumbent on the *baal machlokes* to make every effort to pull away from his dispute, even if he is convinced that he is 100 percent correct. Someone who does not try his very best to end a *machlokes* in which he is involved, even if he is in fact correct, has in essence demonstrated that he is not acting *l'sheim Shamayim*.

Thus, we find that although Hashem had instructed Moshe Rabbeinu to appoint Aharon as the *kohen gadol*, Moshe still made every effort to end this dispute. He sent messengers to Korach to try to make peace, but his pleas fell on deaf ears. Korach and his followers did not take any steps to end their dispute, and if anything, Korach only widened the gap between them. His refusal to make peace ignited Divine anger, and as a result, eventually the earth opened up and swallowed him and all his followers.

We can apply the episode of Korach to our situation today. Hashem, Who loves peace and abhors dispute, certainly feels great anguish watching the rift grow more and more among Jews in Eretz Yisrael. Each individual must make every effort to flee from this dispute, which is arousing Hashem's anger. *Machlokes* is fire, and we have seen what happens when Divine wrath is ignited. Hashem has taken these *korbanos* from among us in order to bring retribution for the *tzibbur*.

When we see such tragedies take place, we must realize that these incidents are a call from Above to stop the *machlokes* and to cultivate love and peace among the Jewish people. Hashem took these tzaddikim from us in order to shake us up and arouse us to return to Hashem in *teshuvah*. If we ignore this calling, we are liable to experience the fulfillment of the *passuk* (*Vayikra* 26:21), "If you relate to Me with indifference [i.e., if you attribute what happened to chance] and do not obey Me, I will afflict you with seven times what you deserve for your transgressions."

This message holds true on the individual level as well. The Beis Hamikdash was destroyed because of *sinas chinam* — baseless hatred — and every generation in which it is not rebuilt serves as a sign that we have not repaired this transgression. Each of us must make every effort to promote peace among Jews and to end immediately any *machlokes* in which we might be involved.

A day before this tragic massacre took place, who would have thought that Hashem could allow such a thing to happen? It was definitely at least seven times worse than the worst scenario of the application of Hashem's *middas hadin* that we could possibly imagine. Yet if we do not take to heart all that transpired that day, and end all *machlokes*, the Torah has forewarned us that we are liable to experience a tragedy that is seven times worse than what we experienced here in Har Nof, *Rachmana litzlan*.

Hesped and Tefillah

I MUST CONCLUDE WITH A FEW WORDS OF *hesped* about each of the *niftarim*.

Rav Moshe Twersky, a great-grandson of the great *gaon* Rav Chaim Brisker, was himself a *gaon*, a tzaddik, a *medakdek* in mitzvos, and a *masmid* such as one never sees, who slept very little during the week and even less on Shabbos, who gave *shiurim* in yeshivah... and who was killed *al kiddush Hashem* wearing tallis and tefillin.

The holy tzaddik Rav Kalman Levine, after staying up late into the night learning Torah, would wake up early, learn *mussar*, go to the *mikveh*, recite *korbanos* as part of the *tefillah*, and daven *neitz* in our shul every day. He would daven with intense *deveikus*. On Tuesday morning after davening, he entered the Bnei Torah shul to ask a *she'eilah*, and was taken as an *olah temimah* in the midst of Torah learning.

The holy tzaddik Rav Aryeh Kupinsky, who was completely absorbed in *chessed* and deeply devoted to the community, learned Torah constantly and pursued *tzedakah* and *chessed*. He was taken as a *korban* while he was trying to save the lives of his fellow Jews during the attack.

The holy tzaddik Rav Avrohom Shmuel Goldberg learned in *kollel* in England, then came to Eretz Yisrael and made Torah the main focus of life, while making his *parnassah* a far less important endeavor. He loved Torah and would learn at every opportunity, loved and respected *talmidei chachamim*, and was taken as a *korban* in his tallis and tefillin during *tefillah*.

We cannot know for certain why Hashem took these beloved Jews from us, but we *can* take immediate responsibility to increase our *ahavas Yisrael* and untangle ourselves from *machlokes*. There is no one among us who cannot improve in these areas.

May our efforts be a *zechus* for their *neshamos* and for all of our people to be able to learn Torah and daven in peace.

Reaching Ever Higher in *Bitachon**

By Rav Moshe Hillel Hirsch, shlita
Rosh Yeshivas Slobodka

W E ARE EXPERIENCING FEELINGS OF MOURNING, DIS-
tress, bereavement and terrible pain in our community. But together with these feelings, there are also feelings
of confusion: Why did this happen? Why here? What should
be done? I certainly cannot answer the question of why.
"Hanistaros laHashem Elokeinu" — only Hashem can fathom
all that is hidden, but the *nigla'os*, the things that are revealed,
are for us. There are *nigla'os* here as well.

The *Mesilas Yesharim* states that one of the reasons a person is created is to stand strong in the face of *nisyonos*. Today
there are many people who live in terror and fear. Hashem
has sent a *nisayon* to our community, to see how we will react
to such a situation — we can achieve great levels of *bitachon*.
Indeed, there is the grief and mourning as we join in the pain
of the families; nevertheless, we must walk away from the
fear, the feelings of vulnerability and hopelessness, through
bitachon. What levels of *bitachon* we can reach! This is the *nisayon*. One of the aspects of this *nisayon* is for us to realize the

---

* This *hesped* was delivered on 3 Kislev 5775 at the end of the *shivah* in *beis
knesses* Kehilat Bnei Torah.

111

strength of each individual and to actualize the strength of this community, to achieve new levels of *bitachon*, new levels of closeness to Hashem. That is the goal of this *nisayon*.

Rabbeinu Yonah tells us, "One who truly believes in Hashem — even if he has many terrible tribulations — will strengthen himself and will believe sincerely that his reward is manifold and that Hashem will give him what is truly good." We need to feel that everything is from Hashem, and not only that it all comes from Hashem, but also that it is all for the good. Everything that has happened is for the good. This recognition is our obligation of *bitachon*.

But our obligation of *bitachon* goes even further than that. As the Tur and Rabbeinu Yonah write: "When a person accepts the Will of Hashem and improves his ways, it is fitting for him to rejoice in his suffering, because there are many lofty benefits to his suffering, and he should thank Hashem just as he would for any success or for any accomplishment."

The *passuk* declares (*Tehillim* 101:1), "*Chessed umishpat ashirah* — I will sing of kindness and judgment." *Ashirah* — I will sing not only when there is *chessed*, but also when there is *mishpat*. This is the highest level, and this is the *nisayon*. How high can we reach? *Chazal* tell us that Hashem tests tzaddikim based on the level that they can handle. The fact that we are experiencing a *nisayon* like this testifies to the level that the community is on, to the fact that they can pass this test as well.

There are some who are afraid. This is natural. When something like this happens, it is impossible to avoid having some level of fear enter one's heart. Rabbeinu Yonah addresses this as well: "And regarding the *bitachon* that we have mentioned: that a person should never trust in a human being, and he should know in truth that it is not in any human being's hands to benefit him or save him, but only Hashem Himself can help him, for all is from Him. And he should know that no human being can harm him whatsoever."

We should feel and understand that the attacker is not the human being (however difficult that is to internalize), and that despite the fact that animals were there performing those horrific acts, the real Attacker is Hashem. When one feels that, there is no longer a sense of fear.

But how does one achieve such levels of *bitachon*? The Midrash tells us that when Yaakov and Esav were inside their mother's womb, they made an agreement: Esav would get *Olam Hazeh* and Yaakov would get *Olam Haba*. Then, when Yaakov and Esav met in *Parashas Vayishlach*, Esav asked Yaakov, "Why do you have so much *Olam Hazeh*?" Yaakov responded, "I have only what I need." But Esav persisted and said, "Let's renew our agreement." Yaakov refused, explaining, "My children are weak, and they can't handle the *yissurim* they will endure from your descendants."

The question is asked: If they couldn't handle the *yissurim* of Esav's descendants, then what about all of the subsequent generations, until today? Rav Eliyahu Lopian explains that if a person lives a life focused completely on *Olam Haba*, he can handle any *yissurim*. Rabbeinu Yonah explains the first step in achieving levels of *bitachon*: For someone who has a strong interest in *Olam Hazeh* it will be extremely difficult to accept suffering. The first step along the way to growing in *bitachon* is to minimize one's attachment to *Olam Hazeh*.

Rabbeinu Yonah explains that "*b'chol derachecha da'eihu* — know Him in all your ways" means that we must live with

Hashem in every situation. Before taking any action we should think, "Is this the *ratzon Hashem*?" If the answer is no, then don't do it! If a person lives with a sense of "*b'chol derachecha da'eihu*," downplaying *Olam Hazeh*, then he can reach very high levels of *bitachon*. The Zohar teaches that when someone is involved with Torah, it is as if he is occupied with Hashem Himself. Once a person has disconnected himself from *Olam Hazeh*, it is possible to achieve tremendous levels of *bitachon*.

This *nisayon* had another purpose as well: to increase *kavod Shamayim*. This community was chosen to stand strong and be uplifted in this terribly difficult situation. Hashem tests a person in order to give him many good things afterward.

May Hashem help all of the *almanos* and *yesomim* to be strong, and may the community achieve the highest levels possible, *ubilah hamaves lanetzach* — may Hashem destroy death forever!

In the Spirit of the Four *Kedoshim,* Hy"d

By Rav Yitzchak Mordechai Rubin, shlita
Rav of Kehilat Bnei Torah in Har Nof

W E ARE NOT ABLE TO SHAKE OFF THIS FEELING OF FEAR — for we saw what happened with our own eyes; that Tuesday, the clock seemed to have stopped — and we are still there, where the four *kedoshim* were massacred.

Why in the Beis Kenesses, and Why with Tallis and Tefillin? MANY PEOPLE HAVE ASKED WHY THIS happened in the *beis kenesses,* and why when they were wearing tallis and tefillin. How is it that the *kedushah* of the *beis kenesses* didn't protect them? How is it that the tallis and tefillin — about which it is written, "The Name of Hashem is called upon you and they will fear you" — didn't protect them?

After that horrific event, a Rav called me to be *menachem* me, and he told me that a Jew whose *emunah* is not strong asked him how *Hakadosh Baruch Hu* could allow such an *olah* to be made — with tallis and tefillin and in the *beis kenesses,* at the time of *Shemoneh Esrei.* The Rav responded, "In order to answer you, I would need to have *Hakadosh Baruch Hu's* permission to answer in His place, as it were, and since I haven't yet received that permission, how can I speak for Him?

"But," the Rav continued, "I have a question: If they had been killed in the light-rail, would it have been more understandable to you?"

"Yes," answered the skeptic. "I would have understood that the time had come for them to leave this world."

"In that case," said the Rav, "I can answer your question: Why should it bother you to think that the time had come for these *kedoshim* to leave this world, and instead of their dying in the light-rail, *Hakadosh Baruch Hu* chose, because of their great *kedushah* and high level, to time their passing to occur when they would be wrapped in their talleisim and wearing their tefillin in the *beis kenesses* at the time of *Shemoneh Esrei*?"

I told this Rav that, without realizing it, he had said what the *sar haTorah*, Hagaon Harav Chaim Kanievsky, *shlita*, said when he sent condolences to the bereaved families. Since their time had come, Rav Chaim told them, *Hakadosh Baruch Hu* had chosen to do it in a way of *kedushah* and *tahorah*. (Rav Kanievsky wrote the same thing in his *sefer Ta'ama D'kra* on *Parashas Chayei Sarah*.)

There Is a Sense of Security Where There Is Strength in Emunah — ONE OF THE REGULAR MEMBERS OF THE *beis kenesses*, who was present at the time of the massacre and missed being hurt by a hairsbreadth, approached me on Shabbos and told me that now he is afraid of his own shadow every time he is in a *beis kenesses*, even out of town. He looks around for a "safe" place, calculating where is the best place to be in order to escape as quickly as possible, in case of an attack.

I responded, "You?! Of all people, you should be the

calmest of all — you have nothing to worry about. You were inches away from the murderous terrorists! *Davka* you, who were saved, should be strong in your faith that the world has a Ruler."

The popular Hebrew saying, "Every bullet has its address," is a Torah concept. It is told about the Chazon Ish that he was once asked about plane flights and the chances that a plane would fall and crash. The Chazon Ish responded, "It is people who fall, not planes."

I once heard in the name of one of the *talmidim* of Rav Mordechai Progomansky, *zt"l*, that during the Holocaust Rav Mordechai was walking with another inmate along the camp's fence. The other person asked him, "Do you still have your faith?" He responded that he had. "But everyone's being massacred — where is *Hakadosh Baruch Hu*?"

"Look," the *gaon* answered him, "twenty meters away from us Nazi soldiers are roaming around with loaded guns, and you surely know that for them to kill two Jews like us is nothing, and yet they see us and don't shoot us. That is faith that *Hakadosh Baruch Hu* is 'just — my Rock, in Whom there is no wrong.'"

The Kedushah of the Beis Kenesses

ALTHOUGH WE HAVE SAID THAT ONE should not ask why this tragedy happened in the *beis kenesses*, *Gedolei Yisrael* have offered, among other things, that since the calamity occurred in a *beis kenesses*, we should strengthen ourselves in our regard for this *mikdash me'at*. And in order to feel the awe of this *mikdash me'at*, we must understand a basic principle:

The Gemara tells us (*Brachos* 60b), "When one puts on

shoes one should recite the *brachah*, '… that He provided me with all my needs.'" The commentators struggled to explain what is special about putting on shoes, so special that the very fact that they are put on completes "all the needs" of the person — when he may not yet even have any bread to eat, or water to drink! Also, why are the words of the *brachah* stated in past tense — "that He provided," as opposed to the other *brachos*, which are written in the present tense ("opens the eyes of the blind," "clothes the naked," and so on).

The Abudraham explains that the reason for this *brachah* is that as long as a person is barefoot, he cannot leave the house and tend to his own needs and the needs of his household, and once he has put on his shoes it is as if all his needs have been taken care of.

The Shelah Hakadosh (and, similarly the Gra, in his commentary on *maseches Brachos*) wrote, "I learned from my teacher, the *gaon* and *chassid* the Maharshal, that this can be explained in light of what Dovid Hamelech said about man and his special status: 'You have made him but slightly less than angels…. You give him dominion over Your handiwork, You placed everything under his feet." This refers to the fact that Hashem created four levels in this world, each one higher than the one before: a) the inanimate, b) the plants, which are on a higher level and take from the inanimate, c) the animals, which are on yet a higher level and eat the plants, and d) the living, the speaking — man, who rules over the animals, eats them and uses them.

That is as Dovid Hamelech said, "You placed everything under his feet": Since man rules over the animal kingdom, he has control over all of creation.

When a person takes the skin of an animal and makes

shoes out of it, that is the strongest indication that he rules over all and that everything is, literally, under his feet. From this point of view, he has had all his needs taken care of, because he rules over everything in the world, so when he puts on his shoes he says, "… that He provided me with all my needs." (In the Gra's commentary mentioned above, he added that that is the reason the words of the *brachah* are in past tense — "that He provided": Ever since the beginning of creation, Man was set above all other creations.)

"Remove Your Shoes from Your Feet"

WHEN A PERSON IS IN A HOLY PLACE, HE is commanded to remove his shoes. Why should shoes interfere with his experiencing a holy place? At the beginning of the *perek* of "*kol hazevachim*," we learn that a *kohen* in the Beis Hamikdash must not have any *chatzitzah* — nothing may interrupt — between himself and the ground. But why was Moshe Rabbeinu commanded to remove his shoes?

The answer is that, yes, in a holy place shoes are a *chatzitzah*, since they indicate the material aspect of the world, everything that man needs in order to keep his body alive — but not his soul. In a place that is *kadosh* a person has to remove his shoes, and at the same time he must remove his control over the entire material world.

Avraham Avinu Rides a Donkey, While Bilaam Rides a She-Donkey

WHEN AVRAHAM AVINU WENT TO PERform the *Akeidah* on his son, Yitzchak, the Torah tells us, "He saddled his donkey, and he took his two servants with him." When he neared the place of the *Akeidah* he turned to these servants and said, "Stay here with the donkey, while I and the lad go yonder. We will worship and we will return to you."

The Maharal, in his *sefer Derech Hachaim* on *Avos*, explains the *mishnah*, "What is the difference between the *talmidim* of Avraham Avinu and the *talmidim* of Bilaam the *rasha*? We find some similarities between what is written about Avraham and what is written about Bilaam. For example, the Torah tells us about Avraham, 'And he saddled his donkey,' and about Bilaam it relates, 'And he saddled his she-donkey.'"

The Maharal explains that Avraham was the leader of the Jewish people and Bilaam was the leader of the nations, but there was a tremendous difference between them: Avraham had a donkey, and Bilaam had a she-donkey. Donkey, *chamor*, shares its root with the word *"chomriyus"* — materiality. Avraham Avinu did not make use of material things; he "rode on" the donkey, indicating that he was above materiality. It was he who led the donkey; the donkey is a male, and Avraham had no connection to it. Bilaam, on the other hand, took a she-donkey in order to "use" it, as *Chazal* tell us. He was connected to matters very much associated with this world and their material aspects.

The Maharal goes on to explain that when Avraham reached the place of the *Akeidah*, he left his donkey and his two servants behind and told them, "Stay here with the donkey." Thus, as he was nearing the holy place he separated himself completely from anything material, since if he were connected to materiality he would not be able to connect to spirituality and would not be able to bow down to Hashem and submit himself to Him. He left the donkey behind, meaning that he left materiality behind.

"We Will Worship and We Will Return to You" AS AVRAHAM AVINU APPROACHED THE site of the *Akeidah* he distanced himself from materiality, but immediately he said to his servants, "We will worship and we will return to you." When he would finish his matters related to *kodesh*, he would return to the material world.

Man arrived in this world with a soul that is *chelek Eloka mima'al* — a part of the Divine, and it is connected to the body; if he would not eat and drink, he would die. The vitality of the body upholds the *neshamah* as well. Although in this world man cannot live without taking care of his bodily needs, he must rule over them.

We find a similar concept at *ma'amad Har Sinai*: "Go tell them, 'Return to your tents'" (*Devarim* 5:27); the *Ha'amek Davar* explains, "*Return to your tents* — return to a life of flesh and human pleasures, as is the nature of man."

The *sefer Menuchah Ukdushah* brings as an aside that on Yom Kippur a person actually skips only one meal, since generally people eat two meals a day, and at the *seudah hamafsekes* a person eats well, and immediately after the fast he eats again. Yet missing just one meal is enough to make him barely able to function.

The point is not that a person shouldn't enjoy this world, but rather that this enjoyment should be controlled and calculated. The ongoing battle is one of who controls whom — who is the rider and who is the ruler.

All of this is true in day-to-day life. But when a person is in the presence of *kodesh* — there we are commanded to remove our shoes. There we are without the donkey. *Kedushah* is, first and foremost, the *battei kenesses* and *battei medrash*, but the home of a *ben Torah* and a G-d-fearing

Jew is also holy. The home of a Jew is a place where the *Shechinah* may rest.

"I Will Be Sanctified through Those Who Are Nearest to Me" IN DESCRIBING THE DEATH OF Nadav and Avihu, the Torah states (*Vayikra* 10:3), "I will be sanctified through those who are nearest to Me." Rashi explains, "*Through those who are nearest to Me —* through those whom I have chosen. *I will be honored before the entire people* — when Hashem judges tzaddikim He inspires awe and is elevated and praised. If that is the case with the tzaddikim, how much more is it so with the *resha'im*." It is written (*Tehillim* 68:36), "'You are awesome, G-d, from Your sanctuaries.' Don't read the word as 'from Your Sanctuaries (*mimikdashecha*),' but rather as 'from Your sanctified ones (*mimekudashecha*)'" (as is brought in *Zevachim* 115b).

The *Kli Yakar* explains that when Hashem sanctifies Himself through those who are close to Him, all the other people gain awe of Hashem. The reason is that if He metes out judgment to those who are closest to Him, then the people who are on a lower level than they are will learn a *kal vachomer* — how much more do they deserve to feel Hashem's strict judgment, as the saying goes: If the fire has burned the damp trees, what will happen to the dry thorns? Everyone will then grasp the message, and Hashem's honor will spread throughout the nation.

The source for the *Kli Yakar's* idea is found in the Gemara (*Bava Kama* 60a), which teaches, "Punishments come to this world only due to [the sins of] the wicked, but when they come, they come to the tzaddikim first." This is so that the wicked will see and do *teshuvah*.

"All of Bnei Yisrael Will Weep Over the Conflagration That Hashem Has Ignited" THIS IS INDICATED IN THE TORAH'S words (*Vayikra* 10:6), "… all of *Bnei Yisrael* will weep over the conflagration that Hashem has ignited."

When calamity hits, *Rachmana litzlan*, the message is meant for all of *Klal Yisrael*, and all of *Klal Yisrael* weep. It is not only a weeping of the many over the loss of the individual. Rather, it is a weeping that comes to arouse the entire nation. The death of tzaddikim is merely a means, with the goal being that everyone will see and do *teshuvah*; and when the entire nation repents as a result of the death of tzaddikim, Hashem's Name is sanctified publicly.

The Disaster Is Meant to Create a "Time-Out" THIS HORRENDOUS TRAGEDY, WHICH SO shocked everyone, had only one purpose: to create a "time-out" in which each and every one of us will stop and think what Hashem wants from him or her, and to give all of us a chance to do *teshuvah*, to sanctify ourselves and to strengthen our faith and our *shemiras hamitzvos*.

When a person lives in a highly spiritual environment and his home is a place where the *Shechinah* dwells, he doesn't need *drashos* and speeches to inspire him to battle the atmosphere that surrounds us, with all its technology. Any thinking person should understand that mundane things — not to mention forbidden things — must not enter a holy place. Someone who has a hi-tech gadget, to be used to store his *divrei Torah*, must not use it at the very same time for mundane activities, and certainly not for forbidden activities.

A person who feels the sense of "Remove your shoes from your feet" will not enter a *beis kenesses* with a cell phone that is turned on. He will perform the act of "Prepare yourself for Hashem, your G-d" and will make sure that he is properly prepared to enter the house of Hashem.

The Home of a Ben Torah Is a Makom Kadosh WE MUST BEGIN TO INTERNALIZE THE idea that the home of a *ben Torah* is not just another household. True, a home is a place where the body returns to be refreshed, but that should be done with control and in a responsible manner; and of course one should make sure that nothing that can harm the sanctity of the home will be brought there.

In the laws of *yichud* there is a concept of "his heart is accustomed to her"; when a person is accustomed to something, his natural "fences" become weak and flawed. Therefore, in some cases that ordinarily would not be considered *yichud*, for a person whose "heart is accustomed to her" it is considered a situation of forbidden *yichud*.

There are people who enter a *beis kenesses* only when they come to daven, and there are those for whom it is like their home all year round. In his home a person feels more free to behave differently. We must refresh our memories regarding the fact that the *battei medrash* are places of *kedushah*, places where the *Shechinah* rests, and therefore one's behavior there should be in keeping with this status.

The four *kedoshim* died sanctifying Hashem's Name. We who have remained behind are obligated to sanctify Hashem's Name as well — all the time and in every situation, but specifically in the holy places. When a person makes sure that his mind is ruling over his body, and knows what his role in life is and why he came into this world, his entire life can become one big *kiddush Hashem*.

In the Aftermath of Terrorist Attacks*

By Rav Yaakov Hillel, shlita
Rosh Yeshivat Ahavat Shalom

Responsibility for Our People

MANY OF THE RECENT TERROR ATTACKS took place in chareidi communities. This is definitely a call to us to recognize our responsibility to *Klal Yisrael*. People are often quick to blame nonreligious Jews, saying that they are at fault for the way they behave. Yet we can infer from recent events that the message is that religious Jews have a responsibility for all of *Klal Yisrael*.

Hashem wants us to bear in mind the words of the Beis Halevi at the beginning of *Parashas Noach*. The Beis Halevi notes that *Chazal* tell us that the animals were killed in the *Mabul*, even though they did not sin, since they do not have free choice as man has. Yet the Torah tells us that the animals were guilty of immoral behavior. How can we reconcile these two statements?

The Beis Halevi explains that the animals were influenced

---

* This article was transcribed by Rabbi Daniel Travis and Rabbi Chaim Burman, as heard from Rav Yaakov Hillel on the day of the Har Nof Massacre. It appeared in the American *Yated Ne'eman* in two installments — one on 26 Cheshvan 5775 and the other on 25 Kislev 5775.

to sin because of the actions of man, for when a person is drawn after physical pleasures and transgresses, he implants that desire into the very fabric of the world, and even the rocks of that area are affected. This is why there are some countries that have become so steeped in immorality that the entire environment has become contaminated and influences people to engage in these transgressions. Thus it is accurate to say that the animals did not sin, for they were merely being influenced by the misdeeds of man.

The fact that society is so steeped in immorality and other evil may well be because of the lack of perfection in our actions. Although we definitely do not sin outright as they do, we must realize that a minor deviation from proper behavior on our part could pull the whole world down and could even influence people to engage in such evil behavior. Rav Yisrael Salanter said that when a yeshivah *bachur* is lax in his learning in Volozhin, a Jew in Paris could leave the Jewish faith. Every one of us exerts an influence on the entire *Klal Yisrael*.

In the passage to be recited before performing a mitzvah, we say the words "*b'shem kol Yisrael* — on behalf of all of the Jewish people." We must recognize and bear in mind that whenever we do a mitzvah it helps all of *Klal Yisrael*. The Arizal (*Shaar Hakavanos* 1b) wrote that before a person starts davening he should accept upon himself the mitzvah of loving every Jew. This affects his *tefillos* and binds them with all of the *tefillos* of the entire Jewish nation. Therefore, if any of his friends are suffering, he should pray for them. *Chazal* tell us, "All of the Jewish people are responsible for each other" (*Sanhedrin* 27b).

The religious community should feel this responsibility for the rest of *Klal Yisrael*. Even the smallest deed that one does with *Klal Yisrael* in mind annuls harsh decrees and brings *brachos, yeshuos* and *nechamos* to our people.

A Call for Emunah* THE *GEMARA* AT THE END OF *MASECHES SOTAH* (49b) tells us that at the End of Days, just before Mashiach comes, we will be placed in circumstances in which our only option will be to recognize that there is nothing we can rely on other than Hashem. We are currently experiencing what our sages described, as we witness attacks on *Klal Yisrael* all over the world, with the recent surge in terrorist activity. Our enemies are even attacking us by driving cars into crowded places, which is something over which we have absolutely no control.

At the same time, however, Hashem has recently shown us many open miracles. Thousands of missiles were shot at Israel this past summer, and many of them landed in empty areas, which are rare in densely populated Israel. What are we meant to do in these confusing times?

We must use both the miracles and the tragedies to fortify our *emunah* and recognize that, indeed, we have absolutely nothing on which to rely other than our Father in Heaven. I suggest that we can accomplish this and at the same time merit Hashem's protection by strengthening ourselves in two areas: constant *tefillah*, and transforming everything we do into a mitzvah.

The first area we should work on is constant prayer to Hashem. People tend to think that *tefillah* is limited to three

---

* This part of the article was a response to a woman who was concerned about the security situation in Israel.

times a day, but that is a mistake. The *poskim* tell us that a person should kiss the mezuzah before he leaves his home and should daven for Divine assistance and guidance both when he leaves and when he returns. While it is true that there are many dangers lurking on the streets, from our enemies who wish to destroy us, we must not forget that one is not free of danger even in one's own home. We must pray for Hashem to safeguard every step we take. In addition to asking Hashem to protect us, we must continuously thank Him for all He has given us — health, family, food and all our needs.

As bad as the current situation is, there are still more people dying in car accidents than in terrorist attacks. We must not be fooled into thinking that there are "safe areas" where we do not need special Divine protection. At times people are even killed crossing the street. Whatever Hashem wants will happen. Our job is to continue to pray for the best and to do *teshuvah*.

Chazal offer us another *eitzah* that we can do before leaving our homes in order to merit Hashem's constant protection. *Sheluchei mitzvah*, people who travel to do a mitzvah, are protected from harm (*Pesachim* 8b). Therefore, we should make ourselves into *sheluchei mitzvah* 24/7. For example, if a woman is going to buy food for Shabbos or to buy clothing for her family, she is fulfilling the mitzvos of honoring Shabbos or Yom Tov as well as performing acts of *chessed,* and she is considered to be a *shaliach mitzvah* who merits Divine protection. Before she begins one of these activities, she should express verbally that she is doing it with the intent to do a mitzvah, for this strengthens her status as a *shaliach mitzvah*. In truth, every step a person takes can be a mitzvah. You can smile at people, say hello, give someone a lift in a car or give a person directions. Similarly, if a woman's husband learns Torah, she is a partner in his Torah study, and this protects her, for one who supports Torah has guaranteed protection.

Chazal warn us not to walk in dangerous places, such as under a wall that is not strong and could collapse (*Brachos* 55a). Such activity can bring harsh judgment upon a person. Therefore, you should avoid entering neighborhoods where our enemies live. If you must be in a crowded place near where our enemies are found, you should take precautions. However, if, *chas veshalom*, attacks take place, it should not weaken our *emunah*. Hashem in His great wisdom has His own calculations and knows what is best for us. Even if we do not understand, we must trust that it is all for the ultimate good.

Following these two directives of constant *tefillah* and making ourselves *sheluchei mitzvah* at all times will definitely build our *emunah* and *bitachon* and will help us recognize that, in truth, there is absolutely nothing we can rely on other than our Father in Heaven. If we fulfill this condition, then hopefully, we will merit to see the revelation of *Mashiach tzidkeinu* speedily in our days.

A Gezeirah from Above

IF, *CHAS VESHALOM*, THERE IS A *GEZEIRAH* and Hashem, in His infinite wisdom, decides that people should be killed, even if they are involved in mitzvos, even if they are in shul or learning Torah, Hashem's Will shall be carried out. No matter in which mitzvos we are involved, all of these assurances become irrelevant.

This can happen even to great tzaddikim. The Gemara (*Bava Kama* 60a) states that when the *middas hadin* is unleashed it is because of the sins of the wicked, and yet it attacks the most righteous first. What about the promise to guard *sheluchei mitzvah*? What about *tefillah*? What about the fact that Torah protects and saves lives? We see from this *gemara* that when there is a *gezeirah*, everything that we have advised here does not apply.

When Moshe Rabbeinu foresaw the brutal death of Rabi Akiva, he asked Hashem how so great a tzaddik could be subjected to such tremendous suffering. Hashem replied, "Be still! This is the plan that I designed!" Hashem told Moshe to be still because only Hashem can fathom why these tragic events take place, and there is no point in discussing it with even the greatest of human beings. In truth, everything is for the good, although the human mind cannot comprehend the deep reasons behind Hashem's actions.

The *navi* Yirmiyahu asks why the *resha'im* enjoy success while tzaddikim suffer. The Ramchal explains (*Derech Hashem* 2:8) that there are two separate *hanhagos* through which Hashem conducts His world. *Hanhagas hamishpat* follows the easily understood rules of good and bad and of reward and punishment as laid down by the Torah: When a person does good he is rewarded, and when he is evil he is punished. Everything makes sense.

However, when it comes to *hanhagas hayichud umazal*, anything goes. There can be a Holocaust, G-d forbid, in which even young babies and tzaddikim are brutally murdered. When Hashem runs the world according to *hanhagas hayichud*, He conducts it in accordance with His ultimate goal. Only He in His infinite greatness knows the reasons behind what happens and how it is all for the ultimate good. At this stage human beings cannot understand what is happening. Thus we see that terrible things happen to tzaddikim, while the *resha'im* have it good. The bottom line is that, at any time, Hashem will relate to the world as He sees fit and for the ultimate good.

The goal of our enemies is to terrorize us and cause us to live in a constant state of panic. In my opinion, the question of whether to place guards in public places should be the decision of the police authorities. If they require that every public place of education or prayer where many people congregate should have extra security, then we must follow their directives. But after all the precautions we take, all we can do is trust in Hashem and hope that He saves us.

LIVING ON

"It is a sad fact that tzaros like this bring us together, that only very sad things bring us together. At such times you can see people wearing all types of yarmulkes, people from all different walks of life, religious and nonreligious, and they all somehow feel connected to one another. Then we feel connected even to people who are not exactly like us — and sometimes who are exactly not like us. But that's the way it should always be. We shouldn't need tzaros to make that happen."

– *Rav Zev Leff, shlita*

Growing through Pain

By Rav Zev Leff, shlita
Mara D'asra, Moshav Matisyahu

Y ISSURIM REFERS TO ANYTHING THAT UPSETS THE NORMAL flow of life. The Gemara teaches that if you think you have a coin in one pocket, and you have to look in another pocket to find it, that is *yissurim*. *Yissurim* make you stop and think. Sometimes the *yissurim* break up the flow of life in very tragic ways, sometimes in less tragic ways, and sometimes in ways that are not even very serious. When we speak of *yissurim*, we refer not only to those we experience personally, for all Jews are interrelated, and *tzaros* that affect other people affect us as well, because we have to feel their pain. Whenever a person experiences *yissurim*, he has to think deeply and investigate: What can I do to relate to this *tzarah*, and what specifically can I do to improve and correct things in my life, that this *tzarah* can give me the incentive to work on?

Feeling the Pain of Others THE FIRST THING WE SHOULD WORK ON, I believe, is to be sensitive to the *tzarah* of the people who are being directly affected by the *yissurim*. This means to feel the pain of the children who lost a father, the women who lost a husband — to imagine their *tzaar*. We must also feel the *tzaar* of those who were wounded. People might forget about them; there are some who are still in the hospital, still suffering, and they may continue to suffer for quite some time.

Chazal tell us that when a *talmid chacham* is sick, a person has to make himself sick over that. We have to feel sick together with him, and this applies not only to *talmidei chachamim* but to any Jew who is ill. We have to have empathy, not just sympathy. Empathy is what *Chazal* call *nosei be'ol im chaveiro* (*Avos* 6:6). It is very difficult to feel someone else's pain, but that is the kind of sensitivity a person has to develop.

The first point, then, is to feel the pain of those who are suffering directly. And if you feel that pain, then you will do something about it; do whatever you can. Those who can comfort the people should be comforting them. Those who can help monetarily should donate to the fund that was set up to help these families. Any way at all that a person can help to alleviate the pain and suffering of those who were affected directly is worthwhile and important.

Cultivating Rachmanus within Ourselves

THOSE WHO PERPETRATED THESE INHUMAN acts are worse than animals. People have called them "animals," but animals don't act like this. It would be a disgrace and an insult to the animals to call those terrorists animals. Anyone who is capable of doing what they did is subhuman. What we have to do in response to this is to hate the evil and to hate that kind of cruelty. Someone who hates it would not want to be anything like that; someone who hates it would want to go to the other extreme. So this should inspire us to want to develop our *middah* of *rachmanus*, to be more merciful, to be more kind to each other. *Klal Yisrael* are *rachmanim, baishanim v'gomlei chassadim*; these are their basic character traits. We are merciful people, we are people who have the capability of being ashamed, and we are kind people.

Every Jew possesses these basic *middos*. And when we see to what levels a human being can descend, what a human being can do when he has none of those *middos*, when he is a *pereh adam*, when he is worse than subhuman — it should give us the incentive to be more merciful and more kind to each other. That is a second response to this kind of tragedy.

The Sanctity of Our Holy Places

THIS TRAGEDY OCCURRED IN A SHUL, at the time when people were davening with tallis and tefillin. Besides the unthinkable evil and cruelty with which the terrorists acted toward Jews, it was a terrible desecration of a holy place and holy objects. The *Zohar* discusses the question of why shuls sometimes turn into churches or other *batei avodah zarah*. This is a common occurrence in America. When the Jews in a city become a bit wealthier, they move out to the suburbs, and then people of other nationalities move into the urban areas that the Jews had occupied. They take over the buildings and the homes, and they turn the shuls into churches. There are many churches nowadays that have mezuzahs on the doors, or places where you can see that there was once a mezuzah. Why does this happen?

The *Zohar* explains that non-Jews could have no power to desecrate a holy place unless the Jews who were there desecrated it first. Because people talk in shul improperly, or conduct themselves in shul improperly, they make the shul vulnerable to the desecration of goyim later on.

This is *not* to say that the shuls in Har Nof were desecrated because the people acted in them in ways that were not proper. We are all interconnected, and in general there are, unfortunately, many places where shuls are not treated properly, where you can walk into a shul and not know that they are davening because of everything else that is going on at the time — all the commotion, all the talking, all the improper things that are done in shul. Among *Klal Yisrael* in general, there is laxity in acting in accordance with the sanctity of places of *kedushah*. Whether it is a *beis medrash* or a *beis kenesses*, there is a vulnerability that is created that enables goyim to desecrate that place.

If we see a *beis kenesses* desecrated, it should shock us into feeling how terrible it is that a *makom kodesh* has been violated in such an appalling way. We should want to see to it that we don't in any way desecrate the *kedushah* of any *makom kodesh* and that we treat our shuls and *batei medrashos* and yeshivos in proper ways. We should have proper decorum there, not saying things that one is not allowed to say there or talking at times that one is not allowed to talk. We must not do things in a shul that are basically *kallus rosh*, acting frivolously and not taking seriously the atmosphere of *kedushah* that a shul is supposed to have.

True Achdus IT IS A SAD FACT THAT *TZAROS* LIKE THIS BRING us together, that only very sad things bring us together. At such times you can see people wearing all types of yarmulkes, people from all different walks of life, religious and nonreligious, and they all somehow feel connected to one another. Then we feel connected even to people who are not exactly like us — and sometimes who are exactly not like us. But that's the way it should always be. We shouldn't need *tzaros* to make that happen.

This is the way *Klal Yisrael* is meant to be. That doesn't mean, however, that we're all okay. There's a mitzvah to give *tochachah*, to rebuke one another — not because I want to put the other person down, but rather because we're all in this together. I want you to do what is right and you want me to do what is right, because every action affects all of us. If that is my motivation for giving you *tochachah*, then I am not doing it because I don't like you. On the contrary, I'm doing it because I love you. And because I love you, I want you to do what is right and to have what is good for you — not what *I* *think* is good for you. If I see you drinking poison, and you think it's soda, I'm going to tell you — not because I hate you, but because I love you. I don't want you to do something that is harmful to you. So feeling close to every other Jew doesn't mean that there is no place for *mussar* and *tochachah*, for reproof and rebuke. It means that *mussar* and *tochachah* have to come from a place of genuine concern for other people.

When there are *tzaros*, when there's a funeral, everyone shows up, all the different kinds of Jews. But we don't have to wait for funerals to make that happen. Through *tzaros*, the *Ribbono shel Olam* gave us an incentive to unite. We can take that newfound unity and extend it to times when our nation is not in the midst of crisis and pain. Then, if we will unite even without a *tzarah*, the *Ribbono shel Olam* won't have to give us *tzaros* to unite us anymore.

We hope that, *im yirtzeh Hashem*, we respond to these *tzaros* properly, so Hashem will see that there is no more need for us to have them. The morning, the *geulah*, will come, and we will see the birth that resulted from all of those *tzaros*, all those birth pangs that we are experiencing now. Then we will look back and see that everything that happened was for a purpose and ultimately brought about that final *geulah*, speedily in our days.

Why *Achdus* Is Born from Pain

By Rebbetzin Tziporah Heller

I HAVE BEEN ASKED: HOW CAN WE UNITE IN THE FACE OF this tragedy?

The best way to achieve *achdus* is to remember that we all belong to one big Jewish family. When there is an attack, we can never know who is going to be there at that very moment. It could happen to anyone at any time. Many people felt that clearly with the Har Nof Massacre. Everyone sensed that it could have been him in that shul, or his brother or her husband.

Achdus comes from a sense that even if someone is a left hand, there is also a right hand, and if there is a head, there is definitely a heart. There are many different parts of the Jewish people, but we are all one body. When the right hand is injured, the left hand feels its pain. This is what unifies us.

The Sforno writes that Yaakov Avinu accepted the concept of *middas hadin*, strict justice. He understood that this is required to serve Hashem. The greatness of Yaakov Avinu was that he was able to accept everything, the whole picture. He took the enormous love that Avraham had and the fearsome awe that Yitzchak had, and he combined them. And from this he founded the Jewish people. As Jews, we must accept that sometimes Hashem needs to pry open our hearts by force. And we need to accept that that hurts.

This is what we experienced with the Har Nof Massacre, and that is why it had the power to unify us. If we want to hold on to this precious, rare sense of *achdus*, of loving your fellow as yourself, we need to hold on to that experience that we all had, where we knew that it didn't matter that it wasn't my husband or my brother (or, in my case, my son-in-law), it was a fellow Jew. We need to feel that pain. Then we can build unity from *middas hadin*, from the ashes of this tragic incident.

Perhaps this is why widows of the victims have spoken out strongly and publicly on the topic of *achdus*. I think that this yearning for unity comes more naturally to women than men because women are usually much less concerned with the politics of the Torah world.

Take, for example, Ezer Mizion, a huge Israeli organization that helps people suffering from medical issues. The women who volunteer and work there come from all ends of the religious spectrum, yet they work together. What unifies them? They all have one goal: They want to ease the burden of sick people.

When there is a common goal and we keep our eyes on the ball (and not on the people who have come to see the game), then *machlokes* will come to an end, even among the men. But the evil inclination is a servant of Hashem and he knows exactly where our weak points are.

If there is *machlokes*, a lack of *achdus*, this is a sign that we are forgetting the goal and are too distracted by the spectators.

We can refocus on the goal by feeling the pain of others,

rather than what we perceive as their shortcomings. This is what Hashem wants of us.

One of the issues that complicates things is that this massacre took place inside a shul, that the victims were Torah scholars immersed in mitzvos. How can we reconcile this with all that we believe about the protective powers of Torah and *tefillah*?

One answer is that we all know we are placed in this world for only a short amount of time, at best seventy, eighty or even ninety years. Eventually, everyone is bound to die. If a person could choose when to die and how to die, there is no better way than to die inside a shul, to die *al kiddush Hashem*. And if we take into consideration how short is life and how certain is death, questions of exactly when and how seem irrelevant.

The deaths of these *kedoshim* were exactly as they were meant to be. Let's focus now on the grief of the widows and orphans; on the pain of the injured and traumatized who have a long road to recovery ahead of them.

Then let's unite in prayer and *chessed* on their behalf.

Our *Tefillos* Can Pierce the Heavens*

By Rabbi Daniel Yaakov Travis, shlita

Salvation through Prayer

AT THE BEGINNING OF KISLEV, I WENT TO VISIT my close friend and neighbor Chaim Rothman (Chaim Yechiel ben Malka, *sheyichyeh*) in the intensive care unit of Hadassah Ein Kerem hospital. I was saddened to see his head bandaged and the area around his eye bright red due to the blows he received from the terrorists. Chaim was in an induced coma and hardly moving, and for a moment I felt weakened by the severity of the situation.

Suddenly I realized how far my mind had traveled from the correct Jewish outlook. *Tefillah* is the most potent medical aid that a Jew has at his disposal. It is by far more powerful than anything else in the world; it has the ability to change any Divine decree.

A number of times in my life I found myself in extremely dire situations, and when things seemed bleakest I turned my eyes upward in prayer. I summoned every ounce of strength, emotion, *kavanah*, and every other ability I possessed, and reached deep, deep into the innermost recesses of my heart. As the *tefillos* left my lips I felt that I had ripped open the Heavens, and in a short time I saw a *yeshuah* from the *tzarah*.

---

* This article appeared in the American *Yated* in the 8 Kislev edition.

The ability to tear open the Heavens with one's prayer is a gift, and in most situations a person doesn't reach this elevated level of *tefillah*. However, each of us must know that we have this power in our possession, and we must do everything we can to tap into it. I turn to *Klal Yisrael* to feel the pain of the Rothman family and all the others injured in the Har Nof Massacre, and in their *zechus* let us try to achieve this level of *tefillah*.

The *sefer Shaarei Orah* explains why *Tefillas Chana* produced miraculous results. *Sifrei Kabbalah* reveal that *Keser* is the highest of the *Sefiros*, and it embodies *ratzon*, the purest form of will. Chana was able to focus her will and touch upon *Keser*, and as a result her *tefillos* tore open the Heavens and were answered immediately.

True *tefillah* is when one recognizes that aside from the *Borei Olam* there is absolutely no possibility for salvation. When a person arrives at this crystal-clear recognition, he has reached a level of pure *emunah*, and he can cry out to the *Borei Olam* with complete faith that there is absolutely no other power in the world.

Rav Shimshon Dovid Pincus once told me that to rip open the Heavens a person does not have to scream at the top of his lungs. He can be standing silently by his *shtender*, and the piercing cries of his heart can permeate Above. The main thing is that he should feel an urgent need for salvation and know that the *Borei Olam* is the only address to turn to.

Running to Shul

MY EYES ARE FILLED WITH TEARS THINKING about my dear friend Chaim Rothman lying in an induced coma in the hospital. However, I know that the best way we can help Chaim is to eliminate *machlokes* from *Klal Yisrael* and to daven, as Rav Moshe Sternbuch, *shlita*, urged.

It is difficult to reach the level of *tefillah* described above without having some sort of relationship with the *choleh*. Allow me to share with you some personal encounters I was privileged to have with Reb Chaim, so that you can get to know what a special *neshamah* he is. In doing so, I hope I will inspire you as well to feel the urgency of the current situation and to try to summon up heartfelt prayers for him and for all of the *cholim* who were injured in the Har Nof Massacre.

I myself was a regular *mispallel* in the minyan where the massacre took place. About two years ago I began to deliver a *shiur* to *baalei battim* early in the morning in our *beis medrash* in Sanhedria, which is where I now daven. Early every morning, someone drives me to the *shiur*.

Almost every morning, as I would be waiting for my ride, I had the privilege to witness Chaim Rotman running to shul wearing tallis and tefillin. *Chazal* teach us that we should run to do mitzvos, "as if we are being pursued by a lion." I do not believe that I have ever seen anyone other than Chaim Rothman fulfill this directive.

Chaim speaks to others in the happiest and gentlest tones. His voice emanates peace and loving-kindness. Just being around him makes one happy and makes one feel love for other Jews.

When Chaim made a *vort* for his son, he made a point of inviting me to sit next to him. Even though he was being inundated with *mazal tovs*, he gave me his full attention and asked me how I was doing. How many people can be so focused on how other people are doing in the midst of their own *simchah*?

After the *levayah* of Rav Mendel Weinbach, the Rosh Yeshivah of Ohr Somayach, I was walking back, exhausted, when suddenly a car stopped to offer me a ride. It was Chaim Rothman, who, in the midst of the great mourning we were all experiencing over the passing of Rav Mendel, felt the greatest joy in knowing that he could perform the *chessed* of taking me home.

One time I hurt my knee, and many people asked me jokingly, "What about '*Raglei chassidav yishmor*' (Hashem protects the legs of the righteous)?" Not Chaim — he turned to me with tremendous sympathy and concern and asked me how I was feeling and what he could possibly do to help me out.

When I came out with a new *sefer*, Chaim asked about it with the greatest of interest and told me that he really needed a copy as soon as I could get him one. Every word that comes out of his mouth is aimed at making a person feel like a million dollars. Who else is there today like Chaim Rothman?

Ribbono shel Olam! We cannot get on without Reb Chaim Rothman! We need him back and healthy as soon as possible!

Please daven with all your heart for Chaim Rothman — Chaim Yechiel ben Malka — and for all of the other *cholim* of the Har Nof Massacre:

> Shmuel Yerucham ben Baila
> Eitan ben Sarah
> Yitzchak ben Chaya

Please also daven for us, the residents of Har Nof and all of the friends and relatives of the victims. We all need a *refuas hanefesh* as we move on with our lives and process the trauma of that morning.

Darkness before Illumination

By Rabbi Daniel Yaakov Travis, shlita

Blackout in Yerushalayim

AN EXTRAORDINARY EVENT TOOK PLACE in our *beis medrash* in Yerushalayim. On the day that Rav Kalman Levine, *Hy"d,* was murdered in the Har Nof Massacre, the light fixture directly over his seat where he learned every day with great *hasmadah* stopped working. Meir Amiel, the professional repairman for the *beis medrash*, spent a long time trying to fix it, yet even after significant effort, and a second attempt to repair and rewire the light fixture, it still does not work.

There is a powerful message here. When Rav Kalman and the other *kedoshim* were taken from us, the world's light decreased. They were such holy Jews that the illumination of Hashem literally shined from their faces.

Now the light has been taken away, and we are left in the dark. The *bnei chaburah* of the *kedoshim* feel the void that they left. What can we do to bring their light back to the world?

We must hear the message that Hashem is sending us. If we listen and make changes in our lives, their blood will not have been spilled in vain. The darkness that they left will be replaced with the strongest illumination.

Returning the Light

THROUGH FALLING, A PERSON CAN RISE EVEN higher, as the *passuk* states, "Since I have fallen, I rose up" (*Michah* 7:8). From darkness comes light, as the *passuk* concludes, "When I sit in darkness, Hashem shall be light for me" (*Yalkut Shimoni, Michah* 957).

We find a precedent for the concept that the deepest darkness can be a source of great illumination in the Midrash (*Bereishis Rabbah* 82:4). It refers to *galus Yavan* as darkness, for Yavan attempted to block the light of Torah through their decrees. Their efforts bore fruit, and a large number of Jews were Hellenized, discarding their faith.

During this period of darkness, the Chashmona'im arose and waged war against Greek culture. Thirteen *talmidei chachamim* successfully defeated the Greek army and re-inaugurated the Beis Hamikdash. So great was their triumph that *Chazal* established eight days of Chanukah as special days of thanks and praise to Hashem for the miracles He performed during those times.

History considers the Greek era to be a period of enlightenment. The Greeks brought art, literature and music to the world — "culture" of the highest caliber. Yet their goal was to centralize the role of man in this world and to hide G-d's Presence. Among all of this "beauty," *Chazal* reveal to us that this was a time of the greatest darkness.

In the end, their attempts to weaken our relationship with Hashem failed. Instead of distancing us from mitzvos, the opposite happened. A new Yom Tov was instituted in the Jewish calendar and another *mitzvah derabbanan, neiros Chanukah,* was added.

Chanukah is a festival of light. The reason the illumination of Chanukah glows so brightly is that the darkness that preceded it was so intense. As *Chazal* tell us, "From the darkness the light is born" (*Yalkut Shimoni*, ibid.).

Strengthening Our Emunah

Jews are experiencing tremendously difficult times here in Israel and all over the world. In such turbulent times the normal reaction is trepidation, and it would seem that we should walk around in fear, lest we meet up with one of these savage killers. Every step should be taken with care.

This is exactly what our enemies want. As long as we feel fear, they have succeeded. They are accomplishing their goal of controlling our hearts and our minds.

Hashem is demanding *emunah* from us, but not the type of *emunah* in which a person merely mouths his conviction to the *Ribbono shel Olam*. Rather, Hashem wants the highest level of faith that a Jew is able to reach — one hundred percent trust that everything that happens to us is in His Hands alone.

During the *shivah*, Rav Kalman Levine's wife was asked how she felt about the fact that her husband was murdered by Arabs. "Arabs did not kill my husband!" she replied. "He was taken as a *korban* by the *Borei Olam*!"

Every time we leave our homes we are faced with a *nisayon*: Will we panic about our situation, or will we strengthen our *emunah*? These are critical moments, and it is exactly during these times that our hearts are being tested regarding their level of *emunah*.

The halachah dictates that when we leave our homes we should touch the mezuzah. As we are leaving we should say, "May Hashem guard my leaving and my coming now and forever." Our greatest means of protection is prayer. That is what Hashem wants from us.

Afterword

THERE WERE MANY SPECIAL PEOPLE INVOLVED IN THE writing of this book. We received tremendous Divine assistance in gathering so much quality material in such a short time. Despite the painful subject matter, almost everyone acknowledged that it was important to publish a book about it, and was willing to lend a hand.

In the Jewish world, we are accustomed to hearing as many different opinions as there are voices in the room. That's why it is interesting that the contributors to this book — a diverse group of *rabbanim*, leaders and various people touched by this tragedy — kept mentioning the same themes over and over again: unity, *chessed*, sharing our fellow Jew's pain, ending *machlokes* and faith in Divine Providence.

These are fundamental mitzvos that each of us can work on today. None of us lacks for opportunities to improve in these areas. We just need to open our eyes to perceive them.

We believe with absolute faith that the Har Nof Massacre was the Will of Hashem. We also believe that this tragedy is His way of sending us some strong messages — and that we have a responsibility to explore and internalize them to the best of our abilities.

Every time we apply these messages to our lives, we affirm that the blood of our beloved fellow Jews, the *kedoshim* of Har Nof, was not spilled in vain.

About the Author
Rabbi Daniel Yaakov Travis

Rabbi Daniel Yaakov Travis is *rosh kollel* of Jerusalem's Kollel Toras Chaim, which aims to train rabbis who are thoroughly versed in *Halachah* and committed to take up positions of leadership and service in Jewish communities around the world.

Rabbi Travis is also the author of *Praying With Joy 1-4*, practical daily guides to improving one's prayers, available from Feldheim Publishers, and ten other books in Hebrew and English. His articles are published regularly in *Yated Ne'eman* (USA).

Rabbi Travis grew up in New York and now lives in Jerusalem with his wife and family.

To contact Rabbi Travis and Kollel Toras Chaim, email dytravis@actcom.com